THE PERFECT
CROISSANT

STEP-BY-STEP INSTRUCTIONS
PLUS FABULOUS FILLINGS
DEE COUTELLE

45,382

Contemporary Books, Inc.
Chicago

Library of Congress Cataloging in Publication Data

Coutelle, Dee.
    The perfect croissant.

    Includes index.
    1. Croissants.   I. Title.
TX770.C67   1983   641.8'15   83-7791
ISBN 0-8092-5498-0 (pbk.)

*To my husband Jacques and Dorothy
Irwin for their encouragement*

Interior photography: Donald Link
Illustrations and drawings: Marion Wognum

Published by Contemporary Books, Inc.
180 North Michigan Avenue, Chicago, Illinois 60601
Manufactured in the United States of America
Library of Congress Catalog Card Number: 83-7791
International Standard Book Number: 0-8092-5498-0

Published simultaneously in Canada by Beaverbooks, Ltd.
195 Allstate Parkway, Valleywood Business Park
Markham, Ontario L3R 4T8 Canada

Contents

Introduction

The croissant has become the most popular bread in America. English muffins and Danish rolls appear mundane in the presence of the coquettish French croissant! This flaky, buttery roll is in demand for breakfast, lunch, dinner, and snack time.

Yet a mystique surrounds both the origin and the preparation of the croissant. This book will clarify production techniques, thus removing both the mystique and any apprehension the home baker might feel.

The origin of the croissant, on the other hand, is difficult to trace accurately. Stories have arisen from many European sources.

The crescent symbol goes back to the Neolithic era; it was found in the form of bull horns in the temple at Catal Huyuk in Turkey. Later the crescent shape graced the Turkish flag, and from this emblem it was to become immortalized in yeast dough. In 1683, it is said, the city of Vienna was saved from invading Turks, and to commemorate the occasion Vienna's bakers created the crescent-shaped pastries derived from the crescent moon emblem on the Turkish flag. In devouring the croissant, the people of Vienna symbolically vanquished their Turkish enemies.

Another romantic tale recounts the exceptional detective skills of the Viennese bakers. Legend has it that bakers, preparing bread in the dead of night, felt vibrations beneath their feet. They uncovered a Turkish plot to invade the city through secretly dug tunnels under the walls of the city. The army was alerted, battle ensued, and the Turkish troops retreated. In recognition of the bakers' heroics, the bakers were permitted to create a symbol of their victory. They chose the crescent symbol of the Turkish flag. In *Larousse Gastronomique,* a venerable French encyclopedia of food and recipes, the legend is recounted with a few minor changes in setting. Budapest is the place and 1686 is the year of the Turkish battle and the creation of the croissant.

A different, less heroic tale reports that Viennese bakers created the crescent-shaped roll, then called a *kipfel,* to ingratiate themselves with their Turkish enemy invaders. As expected, the Viennese bakers have loudly denied this story. Other sources report that the kipfel was created long before the late seventeenth century but may have been promoted after the Turkish battle by a good public relations person. In the 1780s, when the Austrian princess Marie Antoinette was queen of France, she introduced the kipfel to French bakers. Being masters of flaky puff pastry, they derived their own layered, flaky roll and named it *croissant.*

The French, Swiss, Austrians, and many other central Europeans eat freshly baked croissants for breakfast. American tourists visiting these countries have had ample opportunity to sample croissants and have obviously developed a taste for them. Voila! The croissant has come to America. And it seems to have found a permanent home here. Americans love bread in so many forms, and this light, luscious roll, a great accompaniment to so many other flavors, suits our creative urges as well as our palates.

1

The Master Recipe: Basic Butter Croissants

A croissant is a crescent moon-shaped roll* made from a yeast dough composed of equal or almost equal amounts of flour and butter, rolled and folded repeatedly so that 84–90 layers are created, producing a flaky texture, rich taste, and melt-in-your-mouth crumb. A croissant should have a crisp, golden brown, nonsmooth exterior; a distinctively buttery aroma and taste; and lightness or airiness, despite the large butter content. It is a hybrid of crisp, layered puff pastry, a keystone of French cuisine, and a yeast roll.

But how can a roll so rich and buttery be light and crisp? How are all those layers formed? What produces the delicate texture and taste? The croissant is an unusual—and even mysterious—pastry, so it is no wonder that croissant lovers believe these rolls are difficult or impossible to make.

Although croissants may be elusive, they are accessible, and it does not take a master chef's knowledge or years of experience

---

*For ease of understanding, though, throughout this book I often refer to the various shapes formed with croissant dough as *croissants* or *croissant turnovers*, *pinwheel croissants*, and the like.

to create a perfect croissant. The answers are found in the chemical interaction of the ingredients; in the long, cool rises; and in the rolling and folding technique. Once these areas are understood, making a croissant becomes a simple, fun task.

THE BASIC INGREDIENTS

The basic ingredients in the croissant perform functions that help create the soft, supple dough needed for rolling, folding, and layering. *All-purpose unbleached wheat flour* supplies the proper gluten or elasticity that makes the dough easy to roll out. Bread flour with a high gluten strength produces a rubbery, heavy, hard-to-roll dough, while cake flour, with its very low gluten strength, cannot produce a strong enough dough for an adequate rise or for rolling. The elasticity of the dough is kept balanced by the *whole milk* and *salt*, which strengthen the elasticity, and by *sugar* and *peanut oil*, which weaken the gluten formation or elasticity.

Yeast, a most misunderstood and mistreated ingredient, changes sugar into carbon dioxide bubbles, which produce the rise. *Active dry yeast* is recommended because it has a longer shelf life than cake yeast. All of the well-known brands work well. Make sure the expiration date on the back of the packet is several months away. Store the yeast in a cool dry place such as the door compartment of your refrigerator.

Cold, unsalted butter, with its rich fat content, produces the flaky texture and unmistakable taste of a croissant au beurre (a butter croissant). Any substitute, such as margarine, will not produce an authentic croissant. Different bakers use different amounts of butter, but the true French croissant has a nearly equal ratio of butter to flour by weight.

Egg glaze must be painted on a puffed raw croissant just before it is baked to produce a brown, shiny, attractive surface. Additional sweet glazes discussed throughout this book are placed on the egg-glazed croissant after baking and just before serving. (If these sugary glazes were drizzled on before baking, they would burn in the hot oven.)

The croissant dough must undergo long, slow rises in a cool (75°F.) environment to produce the delicate taste and texture of

Although the heavy duty machine is not essential, it makes preparation of fillings easier, and the straight-sided bowl produces an even, full rise. Pastry brush, scraper, ruler, rolling pin, measuring cups and spoons, yeast thermometer, and a cold rolling surface are needed to produce the perfect croissant.

the croissant. Fortunately, these rises can be geared to the baker's schedule. Dough can be refrigerated between steps for a total of 48 hours to slow down rising or to keep the dough "on hold" before or after rolling. After 48 hours the dough can develop a "sourdough" taste.

EQUIPMENT

Equipment for croissant making is as simple as the ingredients. First, use a straight-sided two-quart bowl; this way the dough can evenly "climb" narrow walls as carbon dioxide bubbles trapped in the gluten structure push the dough upward. A two-quart glass measuring cup works well. A wide bowl produces a flat "pancake effect" rise that will not produce airy, light, bubbly dough.

A **microwave, instant, or yeast thermometer** will ensure the proper 100°F. temperature of liquids mixed with yeast so that the yeast will neither die in too-hot liquids nor remain inactive in too-cold liquids.

A **pastry scraper or spreader** is essential for scooping up and folding this soft and initially sticky dough, for spreading butter over the dough, and for cutting the dough. By using a scraper you will need to use less flour during rolling and handling of the dough, and you will produce light, buttery croissants.

Use a **rolling pin** that is comfortable to maneuver. I recommend either a French pin without handles or a heavy ball bearing pin with handles. Make certain the pin is wide enough to cover the entire width of your dough in a single roll so that it is not necessary to reroll over some parts of dough and risk overhandling it, making it rubbery and hard to shape.

A **cold rolling surface** is the novice's best ally in croissant making. When you first make croissants you may proceed rather slowly and handle the dough excessively, making it hard to roll or causing butter layers to soften. A cold surface will keep your dough firm and manageable so that your first batch can be formed perfectly and easily, even if you take a long time. A marble slab or white plastic slab that you can refrigerate when dough is rising works well.

A **ruler** will help you measure the proper size rectangle upon which you will spread the even layer of butter that produces the flaky croissant layers. You may also use the ruler to cut the dough triangles accurately so that your croissants will be uniformly sized.

A **pastry brush** is used to paint a layer of egg mixed with a little water over each croissant as it is about to be baked. The painting of egg glaze produces the even, slightly shiny brown finish of the croissant surface.

Dry measure cups must be used for accurate flour measurement. By scooping the cups into your flour bin, filling them until they overflow, and then leveling them off with a knife or scraper, you will measure exactly the half pound needed for the dough. The French never sift flour as a means of measuring because different sifters often produce different amounts. Measuring by weight is most accurate and constant and is certainly a welcome relief from tedious sifting.

Croissants are not difficult to make. They require no sifted ingredients and no kneading (which would produce a rubbery, stubborn dough). A scraper and a cold surface make dough handling easy. The butter-spreading technique explained in the recipe is a simple way to spread a layer of butter evenly and *only once* over the dough.

The three rises can be planned according to your time schedule. You can begin and then delay the recipe at almost any step, but do not delay for more than two days to ensure a vigorous final rise during baking. Furthermore, this recipe requires only 40 minutes of actual work with the dough. The rest of the time investment solely involves rising time—during which you need not even be in your home. To produce a batch of croissants without using any delaying tactics, you will need a total of nine hours.

So, armed with a little knowledge of dough chemistry, a few dough utensils, and a simple layering and folding technique, you can produce perfect croissants starting today.

Basic Butter Croissants

Makes 12 5-inch croissants (see note)

Equipment
Dry measure cups
Liquid measure cup
Measuring spoons
Instant, yeast, or microwave thermometer
2-quart straight-sided bowl
Rolling pin
Ruler
Pastry scraper

Meat mallet or rolling pin for breaking up butter
Large buttered cookie sheet or jelly roll pan
Cold rolling surface such as marble or cold white plastic
    slab
Pastry brush

Ingredients for Proofing

3 tablespoons warm (100°F.) water
2 level teaspoons active dry yeast
2 teaspoons sugar
1 teaspoon flour

Remaining Dough Ingredients

1¾ cups all-purpose unbleached white flour
2 tablespoons sugar dissolved in ⅔ cup warm (100°F.) milk
Scant ½ teaspoon salt
1 teaspoon peanut oil
1½ sticks cold unsalted butter

For Glazing Croissants

1 egg beaten with 1 teaspoon water

1. Proof yeast: Place water in a small bowl or measuring
    cup. Check temperature with a thermometer. Sprinkle

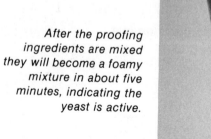

*After the proofing
ingredients are mixed
they will become a foamy
mixture in about five
minutes, indicating the
yeast is active.*

yeast over water. Stir in 2 teaspoons sugar and 1 teaspoon flour. Let stand 5–8 minutes until foamy, indicating yeast is active. If your kitchen is very cold, double the yeast to boost the rise.

- *Make sure the proofing water and the milk are at about 100°F. When liquids below 75°F. are added to yeast, the action will be slow or nonexistent, but if liquids above 140°F. are added to yeast, it will die.*

2. Meanwhile, measure 1¾ cups flour into a 2-quart bowl by first dipping measuring cups into the flour and then leveling off with a knife. This method produces exactly the ½ pound needed for the dough.

3. Add the scant ½ teaspoon salt to the flour in the bowl.

4. Heat the milk and sugar mixture just to 100°F. Check the temperature with a thermometer. Add milk to flour mixture with peanut oil and proofed yeast.

5. Stir with a spatula or wooden spoon just to blend all ingredients. Do not overbeat or you will produce a rubbery dough. Just blend until all ingredients are mixed. The batter will be a bit lumpy and very sticky. Do not add more flour.

Dough in step 5 will be a bit lumpy and sticky.

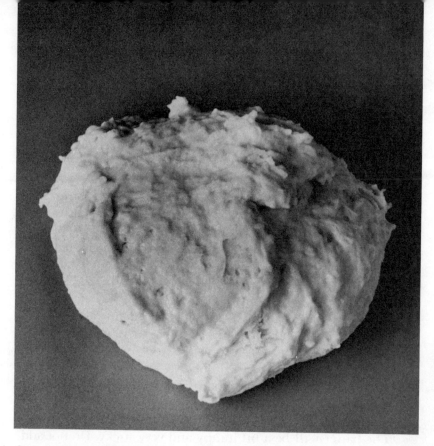

Step 6. Dough must rest for a few minutes so that liquids can be absorbed by dough and gluten can begin to develop.

6. Scrape out onto a work surface and let the dough rest about 4 minutes so gluten formation (elasticity) develops.

7. Meanwhile, rinse the bowl in warm water and dry it. A warm bowl gives your dough a warm environment for rising.

8. Using the scraper, fold the dough in half from right to left. Then fold in half from back (north) toward you (south). Flip the dough over and do the same folding movements again. Do this double folding and flipping four times in all. You are stimulating the development of gluten, but do not overwork the dough or it will become unmanageable and rubbery. The dough will be sticky and still a bit lumpy.

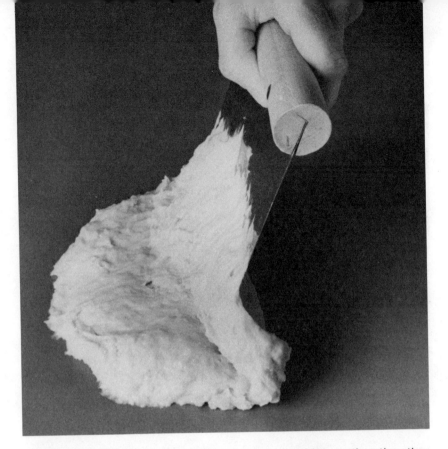

In lieu of kneading, merely fold dough from one side over the other, then from back toward you a few times to activate but not overactivate gluten development needed for proper rising and proper dough texture.

9. Place the dough in a bowl. Cover with plastic wrap and a thick towel and let rise a minimum of 3 hours to near triple in size. Do not put the dough in the oven. A too-hot environment produces a stinky yeast smell and destroys taste and texture. A 75°F. environment is perfect. You can put your dough on a pillow if your kitchen counter is cold.

   • *To postpone the rest of preparation, let the dough begin to rise about 1 hour at room temperature. Remove the towel and place in the refrigerator. In about 8 hours the dough will have nearly tripled in volume and you may proceed to step 13. Alternately, you can let the dough rise to triple volume at room temperature for 3*

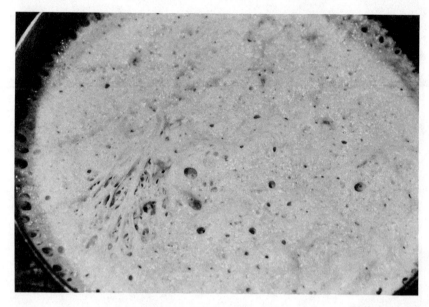

Dough will become very soft, sticky, and bubbly during the first rise to about triple original volume (step 9).

> *hours and then remove the towel and refrigerate the dough for 1 day.*

10. Neatly scrape the dough out onto a floured surface. With floured hands, press the dough into a rectangle 12 inches long and 5 inches wide. Notice how smooth the dough has become during the first rise. Using the scraper, fold the dough in thirds as if folding a business letter; that is, fold the bottom third up over the middle third and the top third down.

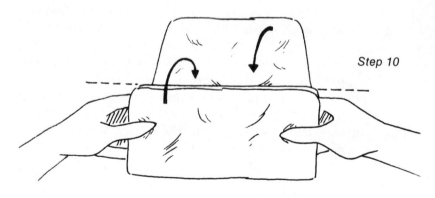

Step 10

11. Place the dough back in the bowl. Cover as before and let rise 1½ hours, until doubled.

    - *To postpone the rest of preparation, fold as directed in step 10, place dough back in the bowl, and let rise for about 40 minutes. Then remove the towel and refrigerate for 8 hours or even overnight until the dough has doubled. Proceed to step 13. Don't worry: In the refrigerator the dough will not overrise in a 2-quart bowl. To ensure a strong final rise during baking, you must finish forming and baking the croissants by the third day. Never leave the dough in the refrigerator overnight more than twice.*

12. Place dough in floured plastic wrap, flatten dough, wrap tightly, and refrigerate at least 30 minutes or place in freezer 20 minutes.

    - *To postpone preparation, flour dough lightly, wrap securely in plastic wrap, place on a plate, cover with a second plate and a weight (such as a heavy can), and refrigerate for 1 day. Dough will get "pillowy," but just slap it while it is wrapped in plastic to flatten it.*

13. Cut cold butter into ½-inch chunks using the scraper. Pound on the pieces with a mallet, a rolling pin, or the heel of your hand until the butter becomes a malleable mass that can be spread or shaped, but is not oily or approaching a melted state. If butter exudes water as you chop and spread it, sprinkle on and blend in 1 or 2 tablespoons flour. Set butter to the side of the rolling area.

    - *It is important for the butter to be spreadable but cold so that you will be able to spread it evenly over the chilled dough without tearing the dough or without letting the butter melt into it. Your goal is to create 2 separate layers, 1 of dough and 1 of butter.*

14. On a floured cold surface, roll the chilled dough into a rectangle 14 inches long and 8 inches wide. The dough will be about ¼ inch thick. Make sure the rolling surface is very cold so that the dough will remain cold and easy to roll and the butter will not become oily or melt into the dough layer. Flour the surface lightly as needed for smooth, even rolling. Use your ruler to measure the rec-

Here in step 15 the butter is pinched into small pieces and placed evenly over the upper two-thirds of the dough leaving the border around dough and the bottom third of dough unbuttered.

tangle exactly and your scraper to help make the shape perfect.

15. Rapidly pinch off butter pieces and place on the upper two-thirds of the dough; leave an unbuttered half-inch outer edge or border.

16. Using a scraper, rapidly and evenly spread butter over the upper two-thirds of the dough, leaving the bottom third and the edge unbuttered. It is important to leave an unbuttered border so the butter will not be squeezed out when the dough is rolled in step 19.

   • *Make sure your dough is chilled. If you took a lot of time spreading the butter, and the dough has become soft and unmanageable, refrigerate the dough directly on the rolling surface for about 10 minutes. In the*

The butter pieces are then carefully and evenly spread and smoothed.
The border and bottom third of the dough are left unbuttered.

Step 16

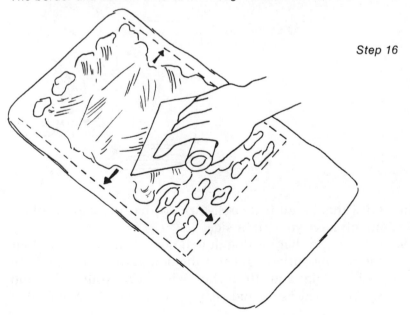

summer or in a hot kitchen either refrigerate the dough on the rolling surface or chill the rolling surface with a plastic bag filled with ice cubes whenever needed.

17. Fold the bottom third up over the middle third. Fold the top third down as if folding a business letter. This technique of rolling out and folding into thirds is called *making a turn.* You have now completed the first of 4 turns that will create the multiple layers of dough and butter, the essence of the croissant. Unless the dough is very soft, go right on to step 18. If the dough is soft, refrigerate for 10 minutes.

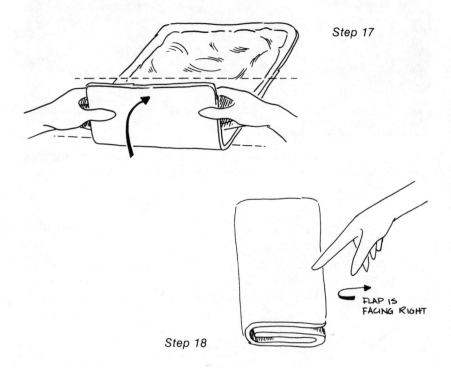

Step 17

Step 18

FLAP IS
FACING RIGHT

18. Give the dough a quarter-turn so that the flap of folded dough faces your right side.

19. Quickly, so that the dough will not soften too much, flour the rolling surface and roll the dough into a rectangle 16 inches long and 10 inches wide. Use your ruler and scraper to measure and shape your rectangle. Notice that

you can see pieces of butter through the dough. That is fine. Again, fold the bottom third over the center third and the top third down. You have now completed 2 turns.

20. Wrap in plastic wrap and refrigerate for 40 minutes or place in freezer for 20 minutes to refirm the butter and keep the dough manageable.

21. Place the dough on a floured cold surface with the flap again facing your right. Roll out to a rectangle 16 inches long and 10 inches wide. Again you can see pieces of butter layered in the dough. That is fine. Fold the bottom third over the center third and the top third down. This completes 3 turns. If the dough is too soft to handle, refrigerate 10 minutes. Otherwise, proceed to the next step and finish the last turn.

22. With the flap on your right, roll the dough into a rectangle 16 inches long and 10 inches wide on a lightly floured cold surface. Fold the bottom third over the center third and the top third down. You have now completed all 4 turns.

23. Wrap in plastic and refrigerate for 2 hours.
    - *If you have not already refrigerated the dough for 2 days, you can postpone preparation for a day after completing all turns by placing the wrapped dough on a plate with a plate and weight on top. The dough will become "pillowy" in the plastic. Slap it to flatten it from time to time.*

24. Place the chilled dough on a floured cold surface with the flap on your right. Roll the dough into a rectangle 20 inches long and about 4 inches wide. The dough will be about ½ inch thick. Cut in half horizontally, making two 10-inch-long pieces. Refrigerate 1 piece.

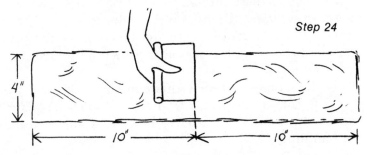

Step 24

Step 25

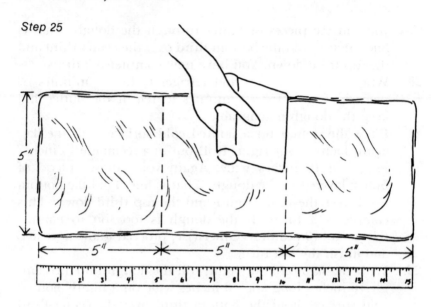

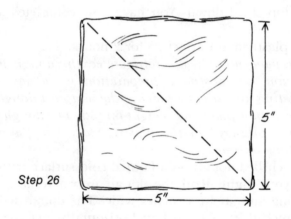

Step 26

25. Roll the other piece into a rectangle 15 inches long and 5 inches wide. Place the ruler next to the dough. Using the scraper, make 2 horizontal cuts in the dough at the 5-inch mark and the 10-inch mark on the ruler. This creates 3 5-inch squares.

26. Using the scraper, cut each square in half diagonally from corner to corner, creating 2 triangles out of each square. If you are working slowly, refrigerate the triangles you are not handling.

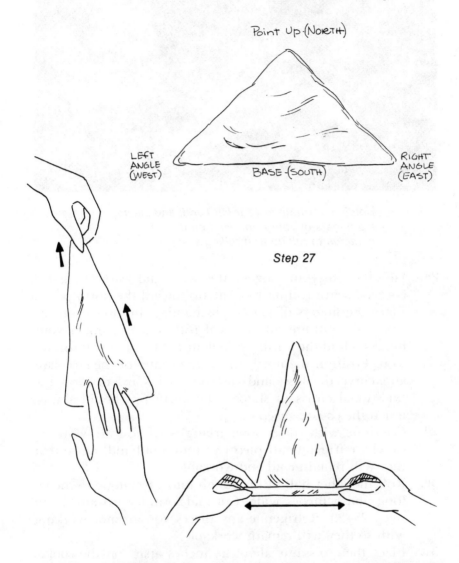

Point Up (NORTH)

LEFT ANGLE (WEST)

BASE (SOUTH)

RIGHT ANGLE (EAST)

Step 27

27. Place each triangle with the base toward you (south) and the point away from you (north) on the work surface. Elongate the triangle height to about 6½ inches by stretching the triangle lengthwise. Using your fingers, stretch and pull the left (west) corner and right (east) corner of the base out about a half inch on each side, widening the base by 1 inch altogether.

• *At this point you could add a croissant filling.*

*Holding north tip in your left hand, and placing
the fingers of your right hand on the roll,
continue to roll up as if rolling a rug.*

28. Holding in your fingers the west and east elongated
    corners, begin rolling halfway up toward the north point.
    Place the fingers of your right hand, palm down, on the
    roll and continue rolling as if rolling a rug under your
    fingers. Hold the north tip in your left hand as you roll up
    to it. Position the north tip in the center of the croissant
    and curve the west and east points inward to form the
    traditional croissant shape. The north tip should almost
    touch the cookie sheet.
29. Continue with the 5 other triangles. If you are working
    slowly, refrigerate all pieces you are not handling so that
    they will remain cold and workable.
30. Roll the other half of the dough into a rectangle 15 inches
    long and 5 inches wide. Cut and form 6 croissants as in
    steps 25–29. Refrigerate any pieces you are not working
    with so they will remain workable.
31. Place the croissants about 2½ inches apart on the cookie
    sheet. Cover loosely with plastic wrap and let rise 1½ hours
    until the dough is swollen and pillowy soft. The dough
    will not rise much during this time. Do not place the
    dough near any direct heat source, for the butter melts
    easily. A 75°F. environment is perfect. Don't place the
    plastic tightly over the croissants, as it could impede the
    swelling and stick to the croissant tops.
32. Fifteen minutes before baking, preheat the oven to 425°F.
    and place the oven rack in the middle of the oven if you

are using one large baking sheet. If you are using two baking sheets, place two oven racks so that oven is divided into thirds. Halfway through baking reverse pans for uniform browning.

33. Mix egg and 1 teaspoon water in a small bowl or cup.
34. Just before baking, brush each croissant twice with the egg glaze for a lovely brown finish after baking. Place the cookie sheet in the oven and bake 5 minutes at 450°F. Croissants will puff and brown in the hot oven. Lower heat to 375°F. and bake an additional 10–13 minutes. When finished, the bottoms and tops of the croissants will be golden brown.
35. When baked and browned, the croissants should be removed to a cooling rack.
    - *Serve the croissants warm with jam, if desired. If you are not serving them within a few hours, you should let them cool completely, wrap in foil, and freeze. If you wrap them in foil, make sure the croissants are completely cool so that they do not "steam" in the foil and lose their crispness.*
    - *To serve croissants that have been frozen, open the foil to expose the frozen croissants' top surfaces and place the croissants in a preheated 400°F. oven for 5–8 minutes to thaw and recrisp. Never freeze formed but unbaked croissants. After being frozen and defrosted, the dough never rises as gloriously in the oven as when baked without previous freezing.*

Note: After your first batch you probably will want to triple the recipe and produce 36 croissants so that you will have some available in your freezer for quick thawing and recrisping. The recipe can easily be tripled with the following minor variations:

1. Triple all ingredients.
2. Use a 5-quart straight-sided bowl.
3. In Step 10, pat the dough into a 20″ x 8″ rectangle, fold in thirds, and place back in the bowl.
4. After step 13, cut the dough into 3 parts and follow the master recipe exactly. It is too cumbersome to add butter and make turns using larger dough portions than the single-recipe amount.

2

Thick, Sweet Fillings

The traditional French croissant filling is chocolate, making the *petit pain au chocolat* ("little bread of chocolate," literally translated). The petit pain au chocolat can be shaped like a traditional croissant or a rolled-up square resembling a pillow. These chocolate croissants are consumed as heartily in France as sweet rolls are here in America. Children in France flock to their local *boulangerie* to buy a petit pain au chocolat for an after-school treat, just as American children consume chocolate chip cookies. The best chocolate croissant I have tasted came from a tiny boulangerie in Terrasson, an ancient stony village in the Périgueux region. What I found memorable about this traditionally shaped croissant was that the chocolate permeated every bite instead of hiding in a solid chunk in the center. (This extra chocolatey taste is achieved by melting the flavored chocolate and spreading it on the dough triangle before rolling the dough into the croissant shape.)

Chocolate croissants are delicious and popular, but chocolate is not the only filling option—not by far. Croissants can be filled with an almost endless variety of sweet flavorings, such as nuts and spices, creams, and a luxuriously thick custard called *crème pâtissière*, which can be flavored to produce many variations. Your imagination will surely inspire you to come up with even more sweet creations. My only precautions concerning sweet fillings are the following:

1. Use only about one tablespoon per croissant so that the filling does not ooze out and burn as the croissant bakes.
2. Never use a syrupy, sugary filling such as an almond pie filling because the syrup will leak out and create a burnt puddle around your croissant.

I have attempted to make the preparation of these fillings as uncomplicated as possible so that you can concentrate your energies on the production of the croissants. I hope you will utilize these fillings in other yeast breads and pastries as well.

CHOCOLATE FILLINGS

Chocolate Filling

Makes about 1 cup filling (enough for 12 5-inch croissants)

6 ounces semisweet chocolate cut into pieces
¼ cup rum

1. Place chocolate and rum in top of double boiler or in small saucepan.
2. If using double boiler, have water in lower part simmering gently. Cover top pan and position on bottom part of double boiler. Let mixture simmer on lowest heat about 5 minutes. Uncover and stir gently to combine. Remove from heat.

   If using two pans, place chocolate and rum in the small saucepan, cover it, and place it in a larger pot of boiling water. Remove setup from heat. After 5 minutes, remove the small saucepan from the larger pan of water. Uncover and stir gently. Do not let steam or water come into contact with the chocolate mixture or the chocolate may separate and become grainy.
3. With a spoon, spread 1 tablespoon chocolate on each elongated croissant, leaving a half-inch border unpainted all around.
4. Roll up and bake as directed in the master recipe.

Chocolate Chip Streusel Filling

Makes 1 cup filling (enough for 12 croissants)

1 cup butter cookie crumbs
4 tablespoons sugar
Pinch cinnamon
6 tablespoons butter
Pinch salt
½ cup chocolate chips (or minichips)

1. Blend ingredients just until crumbly.
2. Spread 1 heaping tablespoon of the mixture in the center of each elongated croissant triangle. Roll up and bake as directed in the master recipe.
   • *You may store the filling in the refrigerator for 3 weeks.*

Note: See also Chapter 8, Chocolate Lover's Croissants, for my Fudge Filling recipe.

NUT, FRUIT, AND SPICE FILLINGS

Almond Butter Filling

Makes ¾ cup filling (enough for 12 croissants)

4 ounces almond paste
1½ tablespoons butter
1 small egg
¼ teaspoon vanilla
2¼ teaspoons brandy or cognac
Pinch salt (more if desired)

1. Break up almond paste and process or blend with a few on-off flicks.
2. Add remaining ingredients and process just until smooth. Taste and add more salt if you feel the filling is too sweet.

Only a very thick filling such as this almond cream filling can be placed in the base of the traditional croissant triangle without leaking out during baking.

3. Spread 1 tablespoon in the center of each elongated croissant triangle. Roll up and bake as directed in the master recipe.
   - *You may freeze this filling for several months. Defrost before using.*

Cream Cheese and Cognac-Raisin Filling

Makes 1½ cups filling (enough for 2 dozen croissants)

   ¼ cup golden raisins
   1 tablespoon cognac or brandy
   ½ pound cream cheese
   ¼ cup superfine granulated sugar (see note)
   2 tablespoons butter
   1 tablespoon flour

1 tablespoon sour cream
1 teaspoon grated lemon rind
½ teaspoon vanilla

1. Place raisins in a small saucepan with cognac or brandy. Cover; place over medium heat for about 10 minutes, until raisins are soft. Cool.
2. Blend cream cheese, sugar, butter, and flour just until smooth. If using processor, use on-off flicks so that cream cheese does not become too liquefied.
3. Add sour cream, lemon rind, and vanilla. Blend until smooth. Again, do not overbeat or overprocess or mixture will become too runny.
4. Stir in raisin mixture.
5. Spread about 1 tablespoon of the mixture down center of each elongated triangle. Roll up and bake as directed in the master recipe.
   - *You may store filling in refrigerator for up to 3 weeks if tightly sealed.*

Note: While superfine sugar may be purchased, you can make it yourself by blending or processing the same amount of granulated sugar for 1–2 minutes.

Cinnamon Filling

Makes ¾ cup filling (enough for 12 croissants)

½ cup firmly packed brown sugar
¼ cup granulated sugar
1 teaspoon cinnamon
¼ teaspoon freshly grated nutmeg
Pinch ground cloves

1. Combine all ingredients.
2. Sprinkle a tablespoon in the center of each elongated croissant triangle. Roll up and bake as directed in the master recipe.
   - *Store indefinitely in an airtight container.*

Filling is spread smoothly from thickest part of triangle base up to tip of triangle.

Walnut Raisin Filling

Makes 2 cups filling (enough for about 30 croissants)

¾ pound ground walnuts
1 cup raisins
1 cup evaporated milk
½ cup firmly packed dark brown sugar
1 teaspoon vanilla
1 teaspoon grated lemon rind

1. Combine all ingredients in a 2-quart heavy-bottomed saucepan.
2. Cook the mixture for 5 minutes or until thickened, stirring occasionally.
3. Let cool. Spread 1 tablespoon in the center of each elongated croissant triangle. Roll up and bake as directed in the master recipe.
   - *You can store this mixture in the refrigerator for about 2 weeks.*

FRENCH CUSTARD FILLINGS

Crème pâtissière, or custard, is a mainstay of French bakers. It is a thick, egg-yolk-rich, satiny custard that fills tarts, napoleons, molds, éclairs, and cakes. To have crème pâtissière in your repertoire is to open the way to endless dessert ideas. Follow the master recipe carefully. Be cavalier during step 2, when lumps resembling tapioca appear. Courageously and vigorously whisk them away until smooth and velvety custard remains. The cornstarch in this recipe produces an exceptionally thick custard which is needed to fill croissants without oozing out. If you desire a thinner custard for other purposes, replace the cornstarch in the recipe with flour.

Vanilla Crème Pâtissière

Makes 1 cup crème pâtissière (enough for 12 croissant dough triangles)

> 1 cup milk
> 3 egg yolks
> ¼ cup sugar
> 1 tablespoon cornstarch mixed with 3 tablespoons all-purpose unbleached flour
> 1½ tablespoons butter
> 1½ teaspoons vanilla

1. Heat milk in a small saucepan to 100–150°F.
2. Beat eggs in a 2-quart heavy-bottomed saucepan about 1 minute, using a portable mixer.
3. Add sugar to the eggs in 3 additions, beating with a portable mixer after each addition. Continue beating until the mixture is pale lemon-colored and so thick that it forms a slowly dissolving ribbon on the surface of the mixture when the beaters are lifted.
4. Gently beat the cornstarch and flour into the egg yolk mixture.

5. By dribbles, add ¾ cup of the hot milk to the egg yolk mixture, beating gently with a portable mixer.
6. Place the saucepan containing the egg yolk mixture over medium-high heat. Stir with a whisk, reaching all over the bottom and sides of the pan. As the mixture reaches a boil it will become lumpy. Beat vigorously for about a minute with a whisk to smooth. The crème should resemble a thick mayonnaise. If the mixture is too thick, add the remaining hot milk a tablespoon at a time until the mayonnaise consistency is achieved.
7. Lower the heat to moderate and stir with a wooden spoon about 2–3 minutes to cook the flour and eliminate a starchy taste in the custard. Remove from the heat.
8. Beat in the butter, and then the vanilla.
9. Immediately spread plastic wrap over the surface of the custard to prevent a thick, rubbery skin from forming.

To Make Vanilla Crème Pâtissière Croissants

10. Prepare croissant dough triangles as described in step 27 of the master recipe for Basic Butter Croissants. Prepare egg glaze (1 egg beaten with 1 teaspoon water).
11. Place 1 heaping tablespoon of the custard in the widest center area of the croissant triangle. Spread a little toward the thinnest point, but not extensively, or it will ooze out and burn during baking.
12. Roll up as described in step 28 of the master recipe.
13. Preheat the oven to 475°F. When ready to bake, paint with egg glaze, bake, and cool as described in steps 33–35 of the master recipe.
14. Sprinkle the baked croissants with powdered sugar, if desired, or apply any desired topping just before serving.
    - *After step 8 of this recipe you can divide the custard and flavor the portions differently. See the following recipes for flavor variations.*
    - *You can refrigerate the custard for about a week, then warm the custard to room temperature and flavor it with one of these variations.*

Crème Pâtissière Variations

Apple-Vanilla Custard

Makes ¾ cup custard (enough for 12 croissant dough triangles)

> ½ cup Vanilla Crème Pâtissière (see master recipe)
> 1 small golden delicious apple, peeled and sliced
> ½ tablespoon unsalted butter
> Sugar to taste
> Pinch cinnamon

1. Prepare ½ cup Vanilla Crème Pâtissière.
2. Sauté sliced apple in butter until soft, about 3 minutes. Sprinkle on sugar and cinnamon. Cool.
3. Add to Vanilla Crème Pâtissière.
4. Follow steps 9–14 of master recipe for Vanilla Crème Pâtissière to make Apple Custard Croissants.

Coffee Chocolate Chip Custard

Makes 1 cup custard (enough for 12 croissant dough triangles)

> 1 cup Coffee Custard (see recipe)
> ¼ cup chocolate minichips

1. Prepare 1 cup Coffee Custard.
2. When cooled, stir in chips and follow steps 9–14 of the master recipe for Vanilla Crème Pâtissière to make Coffee Chocolate Chip Custard Croissants.

Lemon Custard

Makes ¾–1 cup custard (enough for 12 croissant dough triangles)

> **¾ cup Vanilla Crème Pâtissière (see master recipe)**
> **¼ cup lemon curd (see note) *or* ¼ teaspoon lemon extract**
> **plus ½ tablespoon lemon rind**

1. Add lemon flavoring or lemon curd to ¾ cup of Crème Pâtissière.
2. Follow steps 9–14 of the master recipe for Vanilla Crème Pâtissière to make Lemon Custard Croissants.

   Note: Lemon curd is a rich blend of egg yolks, sugar, lemon juice, and rind. You can buy it in most stores where English marmalades or preserves are sold.

Coffee Custard

Makes 1 cup custard (enough for 8–10 croissant dough triangles)

> **1 cup Vanilla Crème Pâtissière (see master recipe)**
> **2 teaspoons instant coffee (in powder form)**

1. Prepare custard according to master recipe for Vanilla Crème Pâtissière. Use 1 cup crème for this recipe.
2. Add instant coffee to warm crème and blend with electric mixer.
3. Follow steps 9–14 of the master recipe for Vanilla Crème Pâtissière to make Coffee Custard Croissants.

Rum Raisin Custard

Makes 1 cup custard (enough for 12 croissant dough triangles)

> 1 cup Vanilla Crème Pâtissière (see master recipe)
> ¼ cup golden raisins macerated in 2 tablespoons rum for 1
> hour or more

1. Prepare the custard according to the master recipe for Vanilla Crème Pâtissière. Use 1 cup crème for this recipe.
2. Add macerated raisins to crème pâtissière.
3. Follow steps 9–14 of the master recipe for Vanilla Crème Pâtissière to make Rum Raisin Custard Croissants.

Chocolate Custard

Makes 1 cup custard (enough for 12 croissant dough triangles)

> 1 cup Vanilla Crème Pâtissière (see master recipe)
> 1½ ounces (1½ squares) semisweet chocolate
> 1 tablespoon rum

1. Prepare custard according to the master recipe for Vanilla Crème Pâtissière. Use 1 cup crème for this recipe.
2. Melt chocolate and rum in a double boiler. Add to crème pâtissière and blend with electric mixer.
3. Follow steps 9–14 of the master recipe for Vanilla Crème Pâtissière to make Chocolate Custard Croissants.

3

Croissant Turnovers

I have noticed that several fine French restaurants are serving small but breathtaking first courses and desserts using thin little dough triangles enveloping savory fillings. The secret of these perfect turnovers is thinly rolled croissant dough. After the well-chilled dough is rolled into a very thin square the filling is piled into the center, and the dough is folded over to form a triangle. Fork tines decoratively seal the edges all around. An artistic cook can even decorate the top with dough scraps. After baking, these turnovers can be cooled, frozen, and then rethawed and recrisped in a few minutes in a 400°F. oven.

You will find that turnovers are very practical when you want to use a very moist meat or vegetable filling that would normally ooze out and burn during baking in regular croissant shapes.

The meat and vegetable fillings for turnovers create a light turnover appropriate for brunches, light lunches, late evening snacks, and appetizers or first courses. Try some of your favorite sauces spooned around the turnovers for heightened visual interest and contrast in textures. Savory croissant turnovers are a refreshing alternative to stuffed pita bread or tacos.

The turnovers housing a sweet fruit filling make lovely light desserts, "high tea" treats, or breakfast rolls. For dessert they may be accompanied by a scoop of French vanilla ice cream and capped with a custard, fudge, or fruit sauce laced with liqueur.

It is important to make fillings composed of fruits that will not exude excessive liquid or become mushy during baking. Pineapple and berries are not the best fruits to use because they contain so much moisture. If you must use these fruits, incorporate crushed macaroons into the fruit to absorb some of the exuded liquid. Use these sweet turnover fillings in *turnovers only*, because the fruit juices will ooze out of a traditionally shaped croissant and burn on the baking sheet.

Whether savory or sweet, having frozen turnovers on hand prepares you for emergency company and lots of compliments!

Basic Croissant Turnovers

Makes 8 turnovers

> ½ **master recipe for Basic Butter Croissants**
> **Flour for sprinkling on rolling surface**
> **Filling (type and amount specified in individual recipes)**
> **Egg glaze (1 egg beaten with 1 teaspoon water)**

1. Cut ½ master recipe for Basic Butter Croissants into 4 pieces. Roll each into a 10″ x 5″ rectangle, which will be very thin.
2. Cut each rectangle crosswise into two 5″ x 5″ squares.

Step 2. Turnover dough must be very thin, between ¹⁄₁₆ and ⅛ inch thick so that the filling will be highlighted and the turnover will be extra crisp and light.

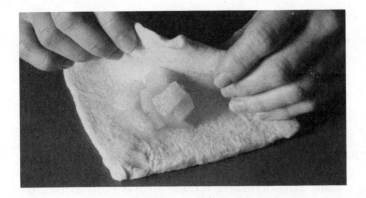

Notice the amount of filling (in this case, chopped pears) used. You can vary the amounts to your taste, but always leave a dough border.

Crimp the turnover edges firmly so that filling will not ooze out and burn during baking.

3. Place the amount of filling specified in the recipe of your choice in the center of each square.
4. Fold the squares over the filling, forming triangles. Press edges with a fork to seal.
5. Place on a buttered baking sheet about 1–2 inches apart. Paint with egg glaze.
6. Bake in the middle of a 450°F. oven about 12 minutes, or until golden brown. If turnovers are browning too rapidly, reduce heat to 400°F.
7. Remove turnovers to a rack to cool slightly.

SAVORY TURNOVERS

In the following turnover recipes half of the master recipe for Basic Butter Croissants is used. You may use the full dough recipe, producing 16 turnovers, if desired.

Polish Sausage Turnovers

Makes 1 generous cup of filling (enough for 8 croissant turnovers)

With barley soup, these make a substantial lunch or tailgate picnic treat.

> 2 tablespoons chopped onion
> 2 tablespoons butter
> ½ pound Polish sausage, chopped roughly
> ¾ cup sauerkraut, rinsed and squeezed to drain well
> 2 tablespoons shredded sharp cheddar cheese
> ½ teaspoon caraway seeds
> ½ master recipe for Basic Butter Croissants
> Egg glaze (1 egg beaten with 1 teaspoon water)

1. Cook onion in butter over medium-low heat for about 4 minutes, until tender.
2. Add sausage and sauerkraut. Cook over low heat for 10 minutes, stirring occasionally. Drain, if necessary.
3. Stir in cheese and caraway seeds. Cool mixture.
4. Prepare the dough squares as described in Basic Croissant Turnovers recipe.
5. Place 2 heaping tablespoons of the filling mixture in the center of each croissant dough square.
6. Fold the squares over the filling, forming triangles. Press edges with fork to seal.
7. Place on a greased cookie sheet about 2 inches apart. Paint with egg glaze.
8. Bake in the middle of a preheated 450°F. oven for about 12

minutes, until golden brown. If turnovers seem to be browning too rapidly, reduce heat to 400°F.
9. Remove turnovers to a rack to cool slightly.

Mexican Croissant Turnovers

Makes about 1 cup of filling (enough for 8 croissant turnovers)

One or two of these turnovers plus a bowl of hearty soup makes a wonderful lunch.

½ cup chopped cooked chicken (drained, if using canned chicken)
¼ cup sour cream
2 ounces shredded Monterey Jack cheese
2 ounces chopped green chilies, rinsed and drained
3 tablespoons sliced pimiento-stuffed green olives
1 tablespoon catsup
1½ teaspoons salsa brava (bottled or made from your own recipe)
½ master recipe for Basic Butter Croissants
Egg glaze (1 egg beaten with 1 teaspoon water)

1. In a bowl, mix chicken, sour cream, cheese, chilies, olives, catsup, and salsa brava.
2. Prepare ½ recipe of Basic Butter Croissants as described in Basic Croissant Turnovers recipe, making 8 squares.
3. Place 2 tablespoons filling in the center of each square.
4. Fold the squares over the filling, forming triangles. Press edges with a fork to seal.
5. Place on a greased cookie sheet about 1–2 inches apart. Paint with egg glaze.
6. Bake in the middle of a preheated 450°F. oven for about 12 minutes, or until golden brown. If turnovers are browning too rapidly, reduce heat to 400°F.
7. Remove turnovers to a rack to cool slightly.

Sweet and Sour Veal Turnovers

Makes 1½ cups of filling (enough for 8 croissant turnovers)

Make these turnovers for an Oriental first course or cut them into pieces to serve as appetizers.

¾ pound ground veal
2 hard-boiled eggs, chopped fine
2–3 pitted prunes, minced (measuring 3 tablespoons)
2–3 dates, minced (measuring 3 tablespoons)
1 teaspoon brown sugar
½ teaspoon crushed or ground fennel seed
¼ teaspoon cinnamon
⅛ teaspoon ground ginger
⅛ teaspoon ground cloves
⅛ teaspoon ground nutmeg
4 tablespoons strong Dijon-style mustard
3 tablespoons pine nuts, chopped (optional)
Salt and pepper to taste
½ master recipe for **Basic Butter Croissants**
Egg glaze (1 egg beaten with 1 teaspoon water)

1. Grind meat twice or have it ground twice by your butcher. Make sure there is no gristle in it.
2. In a bowl, combine the meat, eggs, fruits, brown sugar, ground fennel seed, cinnamon, ginger, cloves, nutmeg, mustard, and pine nuts. Taste and add salt and pepper or more mustard if desired. The mixture should be sweet-sour-tangy.
3. Prepare 8 dough squares as described in the Basic Croissant Turnovers recipe.
4. Place about 3 tablespoons of filling in the center of each croissant dough square.
5. Fold the squares over the filling, forming triangles. Press edges with fork to seal.
6. Place on a greased cookie sheet about 1–2 inches apart. Paint with egg glaze.
7. Bake in the middle of a preheated 450°F. oven for about 12

minutes, or until golden brown. If turnovers are browning too rapidly, reduce heat to 400°F.
8. Remove turnovers to a rack to cool slightly.
9. Serve with Dijon mustard.

Cheese Turnovers

Makes ¾ cup of filling (enough for 8 croissant turnovers)

This filling creates a delicately flavored first course, an excellent lead-in for a fine fish or veal entrée.

5 ounces cream cheese
1 large egg
3½ ounces grated Gruyère or Swiss cheese (about 6
  tablespoons)
Salt and freshly ground white pepper
Pinch cayenne (ground red pepper)
Generous pinch freshly grated nutmeg
½ master recipe for Basic Butter Croissants
Egg glaze (1 egg beaten with 1 teaspoon water)

1. Beat cream cheese with egg. Stir in grated cheese.
2. Add salt, pepper, cayenne, and nutmeg. Taste and season further as desired.
3. Prepare 8 dough squares as described in the Basic Croissant Turnovers recipe.
4. Place 1½ tablespoons of filling in the center of each croissant dough square.
5. Fold the squares over the filling, forming triangles. Press edges with a fork to seal.
6. Place turnovers on a greased cookie sheet about 2 inches apart. Paint with egg glaze.
7. Bake in the middle of a preheated 450°F. oven for about 12 minutes, or until golden brown. If turnovers are browning too rapidly, reduce heat to 400°F.
8. Remove turnovers to a rack to cool slightly.

Spinach Turnovers

Makes 1 cup of filling (enough for 8 croissant turnovers)

This light first-course turnover may even replace a salad when served with an entrée.

½ cup chopped onion
2 tablespoons olive oil
1 pound fresh spinach (see note)
⅓ cup feta cheese
1 large egg, slightly beaten
¼ teaspoon freshly ground black pepper
½ master recipe for **Basic Butter Croissants**
Egg glaze (1 egg beaten with 1 teaspoon water)

1. To prepare spinach, discard wilted or yellow leaves. Then remove the stem and tough tendrils (which produce such a stringy texture in frozen or canned spinach) in the following manner:
    a. Fold leaves vertically, underside up, in one hand.
    b. Grasp stem in other hand and rip it off toward the tip of leaf (removing the stem and tough tendrils attached to the underside of the leaf).
2. Wash spinach thoroughly (leaves are usually very sandy and dirty) by plunging leaves into a large basin of cold water and pumping leaves up and down for several minutes with your hands.
3. Lift leaves out of the water and put into a colander, leaving sand on the bottom of the basin.
4. Repeat washing until there are no sandy particles left in the basin. Drain well. Place leaves in a large pan. Cover and, over medium-high heat, let them wilt. Remove and squeeze in a towel to remove all moisture.
5. In a medium-sized skillet, cook onion in oil until tender, about 5 minutes. Remove from heat.
6. Stir in spinach, cheese, egg, and pepper.
7. Prepare 8 dough squares as described in Basic Croissant Turnovers recipe.

8. Place 1 tablespoon of filling in the center of each croissant dough square.
9. Fold the squares over the filling, forming triangles. Press edges with a fork to seal.
10. Place on a greased cookie sheet about 2 inches apart. Paint with egg glaze.
11. Bake in the middle of a preheated 450°F. oven for about 12 minutes, or until golden brown. If turnovers are browning too rapidly, reduce heat to 400°F.
12. Remove turnovers to a rack to cool slightly.

Note: A 10-ounce package of frozen spinach may be substituted, but I strongly recommend fresh.

Mushroom Turnovers

Makes about 1 cup of filling (enough for 8 croissant turnovers)

Here's a light first course to serve before a poultry entrée.

½ pound fresh mushrooms, minced fine
½ tablespoon butter
½ tablespoon oil
2 teaspoons minced shallots
2 tablespoons Madeira or port
2 tablespoons dry white bread crumbs
1½ tablespoons cream cheese
½ tablespoon soft butter
¼ teaspoon minced dried tarragon
1 tablespoon minced parsley
⅛ teaspoon salt
Pinch pepper
3 tablespoons freshly grated Parmesan cheese
½ master recipe for **Basic Butter Croissants**
Egg glaze (1 egg beaten with 1 teaspoon water)

1. Roughly chop mushrooms and place in a food processor container with the double-edged blade. With quick on-off turns, chop into ⅛-inch pieces.

2. Place pieces in a towel and squeeze out juice. Sauté in ½ tablespoon butter and ½ tablespoon oil with shallots for about 5 minutes, until mushroom pieces separate from each other. Place them in a mixing bowl.

3. Pour wine into the mushroom cooking pan and boil until reduced to about a spoonful. Scrape into the mixing bowl.

4. Blend the following into the mixing bowl: bread crumbs, cream cheese, ½ tablespoon soft butter, tarragon, parsley, salt, and pepper to taste. Add more seasoning, if necessary.

5. Prepare 8 dough squares as described in the Basic Croissant Turnovers recipe.

6. Place a scant 2 tablespoons of filling in the center of each croissant dough square. Sprinkle 1 teaspoon Parmesan cheese over filling.

7. Fold the squares over the filling, forming triangles. Press edges with a fork to seal.

8. Place on a greased cookie sheet about 2 inches apart. Paint with egg glaze.

9. Bake in the middle of a preheated 450°F. oven for about 12 minutes, until golden brown. If turnovers seem to be browning too rapidly, reduce heat to 400°F.

10. Remove turnovers to a rack to cool a little.

SWEET TURNOVERS

In the following turnover recipes half of the master recipe for Basic Butter Croissants is used. You may use the full dough recipe, producing 16 turnovers, if desired.

Apple Turnovers

Makes ¾ cup of filling (enough for 8 croissant turnovers)

Teamed with vanilla ice cream, these turnovers make a delicious Franco-American dessert.

> **2 golden delicious apples, peeled, cored, and cut into ⅛-inch slices**
> **1 tablespoon fresh lemon juice**
> **Pinch lemon rind**
> **1–2 tablespoons sugar**
> **½ master recipe for Basic Butter Croissants**
> **Egg glaze (1 egg beaten with 1 teaspoon water)**
> **Powdered sugar and cinnamon *or* Apricot Glaze (see recipe)**

1. Place apples, lemon juice, lemon rind, and sugar in a bowl. Macerate for 30 minutes.
2. Prepare 8 dough squares as described in the Basic Croissant Turnovers recipe.
3. Place 1½ tablespoons of filling in the center of each croissant dough square.
4. Fold the squares over the filling, forming triangles. Press edges with a fork to seal.
5. Place on a greased cookie sheet about 2 inches apart. Paint with egg glaze.
6. Bake in the middle of a preheated 450°F. oven for about 12 minutes, or until golden brown. If turnovers are browning too rapidly, reduce heat to 400°F.
7. Remove turnovers to a rack to cool slightly.
8. Sprinkle with powdered sugar and cinnamon or paint with Apricot Glaze (see recipe).

Apricot-Pecan Turnovers

Makes about ¾ cup of filling (enough for 8 croissant turnovers)

These not-too-sweet turnovers can be served at breakfast or for dessert.

> ½ **cup dried apricots**
> ½ **cup granulated sugar**
> **2 tablespoons firmly packed light brown sugar**
> **Dash cinnamon**
> **Dash nutmeg**
> ¼ **cup chopped pecans**
> ½ **master recipe for Basic Butter Croissants**
> **Egg glaze (1 egg beaten with 1 teaspoon water)**

1. Simmer apricots in a covered saucepan in ½ cup of water with granulated sugar until tender, about 10 minutes. Drain.
2. Puree apricots in a blender or food processor. Mix with brown sugar, cinnamon, and nutmeg. Stir in nuts. Let cool.
3. Prepare 8 dough squares as described in the Basic Croissant Turnovers recipe.
4. Place 1½ tablespoons of filling in the center of each croissant dough square.
5. Fold the squares over the filling, forming triangles. Press edges with a fork to seal.
6. Place on a greased cookie sheet about 2 inches apart. Paint with egg glaze.
7. Bake in the middle of a preheated 450°F. oven for about 12 minutes, or until golden brown. If turnovers are browning too rapidly, reduce heat to 400°F.
8. Remove turnovers to a rack to cool slightly.

Date Turnovers

Makes ½ cup of filling (enough for 8 croissant turnovers)

½ cup chopped dates (fresh or packaged)
2 tablespoons sugar
1 tablespoon chopped walnuts
1 tablespoon water
1 teaspoon dark rum
½ master recipe for Basic Butter Croissants
Egg glaze (1 egg beaten with 1 teaspoon water)

1. In a small saucepan, combine dates, sugar, walnuts, water, and rum. Cook over medium heat, stirring occasionally, for about 6 minutes, or until thickened. Remove from heat and let cool 10 minutes.
2. Prepare 8 dough squares as described in the Basic Croissant Turnovers recipe.
3. Place 1 tablespoon of filling in the center of each croissant dough square.
4. Fold the squares over the filling, forming triangles. Press edges with a fork to seal.
5. Place on a greased cookie sheet about 2 inches apart. Paint with egg glaze.
6. Bake in the middle of a preheated 450°F. oven for about 12 minutes, until golden brown. If turnovers seem to be browning too rapidly, reduce heat to 400°F.
7. Remove turnovers to a rack to cool a little.

Fig Turnovers

Makes ¾ cup of filling (enough for 8 croissant turnovers)

> 2½ tablespoons butter
> 3 tablespoons firmly packed dark brown sugar
> ½ cup chopped figs
> 2½ tablespoons almond paste
> ¼ teaspoon cinnamon
> Pinch freshly grated nutmeg
> ½ master recipe for Basic Butter Croissants
> Egg glaze (1 egg beaten with 1 teaspoon water)

1. Melt and simmer butter and sugar in 1-quart saucepan for about 2 minutes.
2. Remove from heat and stir in remaining ingredients. Cool slightly.
3. Prepare 8 dough squares as described in the Basic Croissant Turnovers recipe.
4. Place 1½ tablespoons of filling in the center of each croissant dough square.
5. Fold the squares over the filling, forming triangles. Press edges with a fork to seal.
6. Place on a greased cookie sheet about 2 inches apart. Paint with egg glaze.
7. Bake in the middle of a preheated 450° F. oven for about 12 minutes, or until golden brown. If turnovers are browning too rapidly, reduce heat to 400° F.
8. Remove turnovers to a rack to cool slightly.

Fruit and Macaroon Turnovers

Makes ¾ cup of filling (enough for 8 croissant turnovers)

These crunchy sweet turnovers go well with tea or coffee for an afternoon or "high tea" treat.

⅓ cup golden raisins, soaked for 1 hour or more in 3
    tablespoons brandy
½ cup crushed macaroons
2 tablespoons melted butter
1 tablespoon sugar
2½ tablespoons chopped pecans
½ master recipe for Basic Butter Croissants
Egg glaze (1 egg beaten with 1 teaspoon water)

1. Drain raisins.
2. Mix macaroons, melted butter, sugar, raisins, and pecans.
3. Prepare 8 dough squares as described in the Basic Croissant Turnovers recipe.
4. Place 1½ tablespoons of filling in the center of each croissant dough square.
5. Fold the squares over the filling, forming triangles. Press edges with a fork to seal.
6. Place on a greased cookie sheet about 2 inches apart. Paint with egg glaze.
7. Bake in the middle of a preheated 450°F. oven for about 12 minutes, or until golden brown. If turnovers are browning too rapidly, reduce heat to 400°F.
8. Remove turnovers to a rack to cool slightly.

Pear Turnovers

Makes ¾ cup of filling (enough for 8 croissant turnovers)

With chocolate ice cream, these turnovers make a memorable dessert!

> 4 cups water
> 2 cups sugar
> 2 tablespoons lemon juice
> 1 vanilla bean, uncut
> 3 ripe pears
> ½ master recipe for **Basic Butter Croissants**
> **Egg glaze (1 egg beaten with 1 teaspoon water)**
> **Apricot or Chocolate Glaze (see recipes)**

1. Boil the water and sugar in a 4- to 6-quart pot until the sugar is completely dissolved. Add lemon juice and vanilla bean.
2. Peel pears, then cut out tough core and stem fiber. Add to water.
3. Boil the syrup over medium-low heat (so the water is not simmering too actively) for about 15–20 minutes, until pears may be pierced easily with a knife.
4. Drain pears. Slice or chop into ½-inch dice.
5. Prepare 8 dough squares as described in the Basic Croissant Turnovers recipe.
6. Place 1 heaping tablespoon of filling in the center of each croissant dough square.
7. Fold the squares over the filling, forming triangles. Press edges with a fork to seal.
8. Place on a greased cookie sheet about 2 inches apart. Paint with egg glaze.
9. Bake in the middle of a preheated 450°F. oven for about 12 minutes, or until golden brown. If turnovers are browning too rapidly, reduce heat to 400°F.
10. Remove turnovers to a rack to cool slightly.
11. Paint with Apricot or Chocolate Glaze (see recipes).

Prune Turnovers

Makes ½ cup of filling (enough for 8 croissant turnovers)

For breakfast or dessert, these turnovers please any palate.

⅛ **cup dried prunes**
¼ **cup granulated sugar**
1½ **tablespoons butter**
1 **teaspoon orange rind**
2 **tablespoons shredded coconut**
½ **master recipe for Basic Butter Croissants**
Egg glaze (1 egg beaten with 1 teaspoon water)

1. Simmer prunes in a covered saucepan in ½ cup of water with the sugar until tender, about 10 minutes. Drain well.
2. Puree prunes in blender or food processor.
3. Mix prunes with butter, orange rind, and coconut. Let cool.
4. Prepare 8 dough squares as described in the Basic Croissant Turnovers recipe.
5. Place 1 tablespoon of filling in the center of each croissant dough square.
6. Fold the squares over the filling, forming triangles. Press edges with a fork to seal.
7. Place on a greased cookie sheet about 2 inches apart. Paint with egg glaze.
8. Bake in the middle of a preheated 450° F. oven for about 12 minutes, or until golden brown. If turnovers are browning too rapidly, reduce heat to 400° F.
9. Remove turnovers to a rack to cool slightly.

Poppy Seed Turnovers

Makes ½ cup of filling (enough for 8 croissant turnovers)

With tea or coffee, these turnovers meet the requirements of any sweet tooth.

> 3 tablespoons poppy seeds
> 1 teaspoon butter
> 2 tablespoons powdered sugar
> 2¼ teaspoons honey
> ½ teaspoon grated orange rind
> ¼ cup dark seedless raisins
> 1 small egg white, stiffly beaten
> ½ master recipe for Basic Butter Croissants
> Egg glaze (1 egg beaten with 1 teaspoon water)

1. Crush poppy seeds in a blender or food processor.
2. Melt butter in a small skillet. Add ground poppy seeds, cooking and stirring about 4 minutes over medium heat.
3. Stir in powdered sugar, honey, orange rind, and raisins.
4. Fold mixture into stiffly beaten egg white.
5. Prepare 8 dough squares as described in the Basic Croissant Turnovers recipe.
6. Place 1 tablespoon of filling in the center of each croissant dough square.
7. Fold the squares over the filling, forming triangles. Press edges with a fork to seal.
8. Place on a greased cookie sheet about 2 inches apart. Paint with egg glaze.
9. Bake in the middle of a preheated 450°F. oven for about 12 minutes, until golden brown. If turnovers seem to be browning too rapidly, reduce heat to 400°F.
10. Remove turnovers to a rack to cool slightly.

Sweet Cheese Turnovers

Makes ¾ cup of filling (enough for 8 croissant turnovers)

After a light entrée these creamy, rich turnovers make a luscious dessert, perhaps rivaling cheesecake!

5 ounces cream cheese
7 tablespoons superfine granulated sugar (see note)
1 large egg
½ teaspoon vanilla extract and ½ teaspoon orange flower
 water *or* 1 teaspoon vanilla extract
½ master recipe for Basic Butter Croissants
Egg glaze (1 egg beaten with 1 teaspoon water)
Powdered sugar

1. Beat cream cheese with sugar.
2. Add the egg and beat until blended.
3. Add vanilla or blend of vanilla and orange flower water.
4. Prepare 8 dough squares as described in the Basic Croissant Turnovers recipe.
5. Place 1½ tablespoons of filling in the center of each croissant dough square.
6. Fold the squares over the filling, forming triangles. Press edges with a fork to seal.
7. Place on a buttered or greased baking sheet about 2 inches apart. Paint with egg glaze.
8. Bake in the middle of a preheated 450°F. oven for about 12 minutes, or until golden brown. If turnovers are browning too rapidly, reduce heat to 400°F.
9. Remove turnovers to a rack to cool slightly.
10. Sprinkle with powdered sugar through a sieve.

Note: While superfine sugar may be purchased, you can make it yourself by blending or processing the same amount of granulated sugar for 1–2 minutes.

4

Glazes and Toppings

These glazes and toppings add interest and flavor to your croissants. They serve a practical purpose, too; if you are serving a variety of croissants, you can identify the filling flavors by using a particular topping with a particular filling.

You must use these glazes and toppings only on a completely baked or completely recrisped croissant, or the sugar in the toppings will burn as the croissants are heated. The following table offers suggested combinations of croissants or turnovers and toppings.

Filling	Toppings
Almond Butter	Apricot Glaze
Apple	Almond Glaze/Apricot Glaze
Apple Vanilla Custard	Simple Glaze
Apricot-Pecan	Cream Topping/Slivered Almond
Cheese	Crunchy Topping
Chocolate	Chocolate Glaze/Powdered sugar and cream
Chocolate Chip Streusel	Chocolate Glaze/Peanut Butter Topping
Chocolate Custard	Chocolate Glaze
Cinnamon	Simple Glaze
Coffee Chocolate Chip Custard	Chocolate Glaze
Coffee Custard	Simple Glaze

Filling	Toppings
Cream Cheese and Cognac-Raisin	Powdered sugar
Date	Slivered Almond/Powdered sugar
Egg Roll	Honey Glaze/Dijon mustard
Fig	Slivered Almond/Powdered sugar
Fruit and Macaroon	Almond Glaze
Ham and Cheese	Honey
Lemon Custard	Lemon Topping
Mexican	Crunchy Topping
Mushroom	Sauce 2 for Chicken en Croute
Pear	Chocolate Glaze/Cream Topping
Pepperoni and Mozzarella	Crunchy Topping
Polish Sausage	Crunchy Topping/Mayonnaise
Poppy Seed	Cream Topping/Apricot Glaze
Prune	Cream Topping
Rum Raisin Custard	Simple Glaze
Spinach	Crunchy Topping/Dijon mustard/Sauce 2 for Chicken en Croute
Sweet and Sour Veal	Apricot Glaze/Dijon mustard/Mayonnaise
Vanilla Crème Pâtissière	Peanut Butter Glaze/Chocolate Glaze/Almond Glaze/Powdered sugar
Walnut Raisin	Simple Glaze

CREME FRAICHE

Crème fraîche is another basic French ingredient used in rich cream sauces for veal, chicken, and fish; in custards and sweet dessert sauces. This cream, containing natural lactic acids and ferments, will thicken at room temperature and develop a

Crème
Fraîche..

nutlike, slightly bitter flavor. When added to a cream recipe it imparts its flavor and rich consistency. It boils without curdling and lasts in your refrigerator for up to three weeks.

Crème fraîche is used in several glaze and topping recipes in this chapter. Following are two recipes for preparing it. Choose one based on the ingredients you have on hand in your refrigerator.

Crème Fraîche 1

Makes 1½ cups crème fraîche

1 cup whipping cream (see note)
½ cup buttermilk

1. Place cream and buttermilk in 1-quart saucepan. Heat to 85–90°F., whisking to blend.
2. Pour into a wide-mouthed jar or plastic container. Leaving cover askew, let jar remain at room temperature for 12 hours.
3. Stir to blend. Cover securely and refrigerate.
   - *Crème fraîche will keep for about 1–2 weeks.*

   Note: Buy the kind of cream that does not say "ultrapasteurized." Ultrapasteurization destroys some ferments that are needed to thicken the crème fraîche.

Crème Fraîche 2

Makes 2½ cups crème fraîche

1 pint Half and Half
½ cup sour cream

1. Place Half and Half and sour cream in a 2-quart saucepan. Heat to 85–90°F., whisking to blend.
2. Pour into a wide-mouthed jar. Leaving cover askew, let jar remain at room temperature for 12 hours.
3. Stir to blend. Cover securely and refrigerate.
   - *Crème fraîche will keep for about 1–2 weeks.*

GLAZES

Simple Glaze

Makes ¾ cup of glaze (enough for 12 croissants)

1 cup powdered sugar, sifted directly into measuring cup
4–6 teaspoons water

1. Combine ingredients, beginning with 4 teaspoons of water, and adding more as needed to create a drizzling consistency.
2. Drizzle over warm croissants.

Honey Glaze

Makes ⅓ cup of glaze (enough for 12 croissants)

1 tablespoon sugar
1 tablespoon water
¼ cup honey

1. Combine ingredients in 1-quart saucepan. Heat to a boil. Reduce heat to low and cook for 3 minutes.
2. Cool and spoon sparingly over warm croissants.

Almond Glaze

Makes ¾ cup of glaze (enough for 12 croissants)

> **1 cup powdered sugar, sifted directly into measuring cup**
> **2 tablespoons soft butter**
> **3–4 tablespoons milk**
> **½ teaspoon almond extract**

1. Blend all ingredients, starting with 3 tablespoons of milk and adding more, if necessary, to make a mixture of drizzling consistency.
2. Drizzle over warm croissants.

Chocolate Glaze

Makes ¾ cup of glaze (enough for 12 croissants)

> **4 ounces semisweet chocolate, cut into pieces**
> **¼ cup Crème Fraîche 1 or 2 (see recipes)**
> **¼ cup light corn syrup**

1. Combine all ingredients in 1-quart saucepan.
2. Stir over medium heat until chocolate is melted and mixture is smooth.
3. Spread over barely warm or cooled croissants.

Peanut Butter Glaze

Makes ½ cup of glaze (enough for 12 croissants)

> **⅓ cup powdered sugar, measured and then sifted into a bowl**
> **5 teaspoons peanut butter at room temperature**
> **1½ teaspoons honey**
> **4–6 teaspoons milk**
> **3 tablespoons chopped peanuts**

1. Combine all ingredients except peanuts. Begin with 4 teaspoons of milk, adding more to create a drizzling consistency.
2. Drizzle over warm croissants.
3. Sprinkle with peanuts.

Cream Topping

Makes ¾ cup of topping (enough for 12 croissants)

½ cup sugar
2 tablespoons Crème Fraîche 1 or 2 (see recipes) or Half and Half
2 teaspoons butter
½ teaspoon vanilla
1 egg, slightly beaten

1. Combine all ingredients in 1-quart saucepan.
2. Cook, stirring constantly, over medium-low heat until smooth and thickened.
3. Let topping cool until it is the proper consistency for spreading on cool croissants.

Lemon Topping

Makes ¾ cup of topping (enough for 12 croissants)

1 cup powdered sugar, sifted directly into measuring cup
2-3 tablespoons milk
1 teaspoon lemon extract

1. Combine sugar, 2 tablespoons milk, and lemon extract in a small mixing bowl. Beat with whisk or electric mixer until smooth. Add more milk if needed.
2. Spread smoothly over warm or cool croissants.

Apricot Glaze

Makes 1½–1¾ cups of glaze (enough for 24 croissants)

> **1 17-ounce jar apricot preserves**
> **2 tablespoons sugar**

1. Push apricot preserves through a sieve into heavy-bottomed 1-quart saucepan. Discard solid pieces.
2. Add sugar. Let mixture come to a boil. Simmer for about 8 minutes, until mixture passes this consistency test: Sandwich a little of the mixture between your thumb and first finger. As you slowly separate your thumb and finger by 1 inch, the mixture should form a thin string connecting the two. Let cool slightly. Spread on warm or cool croissants.
   - *Store mixture in a jar in the refrigerator, where it can remain indefinitely. Reheat before each use.*

Slivered Almond Topping

Makes ¾–1 cup of topping (enough for 12 croissants)

> **⅓ cup sugar**
> **⅓ cup butter**
> **1 tablespoon milk**
> **½ cup slivered almonds**
> **¼ teaspoon almond extract**

1. In 1-quart saucepan, heat sugar, butter, and milk to a boil, stirring constantly. Boil 1 minute.
2. Remove from heat. Stir in almond slivers and almond extract.
3. Cool until spreadable.
4. Spread over warm croissants.

Crunchy Topping for Meat-Filled Croissant Turnovers

Makes 1 cup of topping (enough for 16 croissant turnovers)

1 cup herb-seasoned croutons

1. Place croutons in a blender or food processor, and process until crushed and crumbly.
2. After meat-filled croissant turnovers are painted with egg glaze, gently press on 1 tablespoon topping.
3. Bake as directed.

Sugar/Decorative Toppings

Place powdered sugar in a sieve and shake gently over warm or cool croissants.

For variety, you can shake cocoa over powdered sugar.

For holiday entertaining, you may sprinkle chocolate shot, shavings, or sparkling sugars over any topping or glaze.

5

Other Roles for Croissants and Croissant Dough

We eat first with our eyes. Just the appearance of food arranged on a plate arouses or depresses our appetites, so a lovely presentation of food contributes greatly to the enjoyment of the food. Croissants are certainly lovely to behold and enhance any food with which they are teamed. The buttery rich taste and light, flaky texture complement both sweet and savory foods. Even leftovers become exciting new entrées when accompanied by or wrapped in croissant dough.

In this chapter you will learn new roles this versatile dough can play. Besides being split and used to house any lunch meat or cheese, you can present them open-faced and smothered with such delicate entrées as Scallops in Cream. Or, as a fresh and colorful luncheon treat, pile them with a chicken, bean sprout, and red grape combination salad. Any of your favorite salads or stews take on a new look when presented on a croissant.

Croissant dough baked into three rectangles becomes crisp layers to be slathered with two salad fillings in between. These layered sandwiches, cut vertically, are lovely luncheon or even bridal shower specialties. Using this dough to make a tart shell shows off your best creamed meat filling and the crisp, buttery dough that will *not* get soggy, even with liquidy fillings. Another attractive use for this dough is as a wrapping for a beautiful piece of beef or even sausage. The meat remains juicy but not stewed, and the croissant dough will cook but will not become soggy.

These additional uses of croissant dough are suggestions or springboards. Use your imagination and creativity to reconstruct some old recipes or utilize favorite fillings in new croissant coverings.

OPEN-FACED CROISSANT SANDWICHES

Open-faced croissant sandwiches made from baked croissants that have been split horizontally and then topped with a colorful sandwich filling create a lovely plate. Splitting the croissant horizontally highlights the layered texture and rich buttery color.

Both hot and cold sandwich fillings work well with the crisp, buttery croissant. The contrast in textures as well as flavors when the filling has a sauce with it is bound to bring raves.

Only a few recipes for open-faced croissant sandwich fillings are presented here in the expectation that many other recipes from your repertoire can be adapted to this delightful variation on the everyday sandwich.

California Chicken Salad Sandwiches

Makes 3 cups of filling (enough for 6–8 croissant sandwiches)

> ¼ cup Processor Mayonnaise (see recipe)
> ¼ cup yogurt
> 2 teaspoons orange juice concentrate, thawed and undiluted
> ¼ teaspoon salt
> ¼ teaspoon tarragon
> Pinch white pepper
> ¼ teaspoon ground ginger
> 2 cups cubed cooked chicken
> 1 cup red seedless grapes, halved
> ½ cup bean sprouts
> Gherkin slices or finely minced parsley for decoration
> 6–8 croissants, baked and split horizontally

1. In a large bowl, mix mayonnaise, yogurt, orange juice concentrate, salt, tarragon, pepper, and ginger.
2. Add chicken, grapes, and bean sprouts. Toss gently.
3. Place about ½ cup attractively on bottom half of split croissant. Decorate with gherkins or parsley. Place cover half next to bottom half, cut side down. Repeat with remaining croissants.

Sloppy Joe Sandwiches

Makes 2½ cups of filling (enough for 6–8 croissant sandwiches)

> 1 pound lean ground beef
> ½ cup chopped onion
> ½ teaspoon salt
> 1 cup catsup
> 1 teaspoon Dijon mustard
> ½ teaspoon chili powder
> Pinch cumin
> ¼ cup chopped celery

¼ cup chopped sweet red pepper
¼ cup chopped zucchini
6–8 croissants, baked and split horizontally

1. In a 10-inch skillet, lightly brown the beef for 3 minutes, stirring often. Add onion and salt. Cook about 8 minutes, or until onions are soft.
2. Drain fat. Add catsup, mustard, chili powder, and cumin to skillet.
3. Simmer 15 minutes on low heat.
4. Add celery, red pepper, and zucchini. Heat 5 minutes.
5. Spoon over bottom halves of croissants. Place top halves attractively askew on each.

Italian Roast Beef Sandwiches

Makes 2 cups of filling (enough for 6 croissant sandwiches)

½ cup sliced Italian plum tomatoes
½ cup chopped green or red pepper
½ cup thinly sliced cucumber
½ cup sliced raw mushrooms
¼ cup thinly sliced green onion (white part only)
¼ cup Italian dressing (bottled or homemade)
6 large Boston or romaine lettuce leaves
6 baked and split croissants
6 thin slices of roast beef
6 tablespoons grated Parmesan cheese

1. In a large bowl, combine tomatoes, pepper, cucumber, mushrooms, and green onion.
2. Add dressing and toss gently.
3. Place a lettuce leaf on each bottom croissant half. Top each with a slice of roast beef.
4. Top with vegetables and sprinkle with Parmesan cheese.
5. Place top half of croissant next to bottom half, cut side down.

Scallops-in-Cream Sandwiches

Makes 6 servings (using 6 baked and split croissants)

 1 cup dry vermouth
 ½ teaspoon salt
 Pinch white pepper
 1 bay leaf
 3 tablespoons minced shallots
 1 pound scallops, rinsed
 ½ pound fresh mushrooms, sliced

Sauce
 3 tablespoons salted butter
 4 tablespoons flour
 ¾ cup milk
 2 egg yolks
 ½ cup whipping cream, Crème Fraîche, or Milnot
 Salt, white pepper, lemon juice, sugar to taste

Topping
 6 tablespoons grated Swiss cheese
 1½ tablespoons butter

 6 baked and split croissants

1. Simmer wine and flavorings for 5 minutes in 3- to 4-quart saucepan or casserole.
2. Add scallops and mushrooms. Add enough water barely to cover ingredients.
3. Bring to a simmer (begin with high heat, watch carefully, then reduce heat). Simmer slowly, covered, for 5 minutes.
4. Remove scallops and mushrooms. Set aside. Reduce poaching liquid to 1 cup.
5. Cook butter and flour slowly in heavy 2-quart saucepan, letting them foam for about 2 minutes. Off heat, beat in the reduced 1 cup of poaching liquid. Add milk and boil for 1 minute. Blend yolks and cream or Milnot in a bowl. Add driblets of hot sauce until you have added about ¾ cup. Return everything to the saucepan and boil, stirring, for 1

minute. Thin out with extra cream or Milnot. Season with salt, pepper, lemon juice. Strain.

6. Butter a baking dish. Cut scallops into bite-sized pieces. Blend two-thirds of the sauce with scallops and mushrooms. Spoon mixture into dish. Cover with rest of sauce. Sprinkle with cheese and butter cut into bits.

7. Refrigerate until ready to make final preparations.

8. Bring to room temperature or heat until warm on top of stove. Place under broiler (about 400°F.) about 8–9 inches from heating unit or coil and broil about 12–15 minutes to heat through gradually and brown top. Spoon one-sixth of the scallop and cream mixture over the bottom of each split baked croissant. Place top sections attractively askew on each.

- *You can put the recipe together through step 7 the night before serving it. Make sure you drain the cooked scallops and mushrooms well before mixing with the sauce.*

LAYERED CROISSANT SANDWICHES

Three crisp rectangles of croissant dough in lieu of bread make an unusual variation of the traditional long layered sandwich log. Cream cheese or any firm salad filling housed

Layered Croissant Sandwiches can be constructed with any of your favorite cold salad fillings to create a "three-story" sensation.

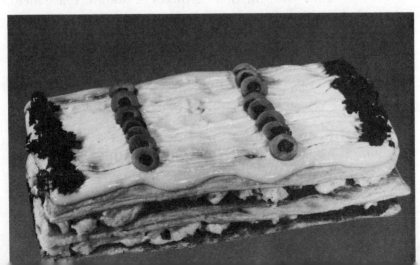

between the croissant rectangles can be used to create an unusual appetizer or light lunch fare when the sandwich log is sliced vertically. Chicken, tuna, turkey, crab meat, shrimp, or egg salad layers complement the crispy layers of croissant dough. Included in this section are some salad recipes as well as a recipe for homemade mayonnaise to bind the salad or to decorate the top of the layered croissant sandwiches.

Layered Croissant Sandwiches

Makes 12 servings

> 1 master recipe for **Basic Butter Croissants**
> Egg glaze (1 egg beaten with 1 teaspoon water)
> About 2 cups each of 2 kinds of cold salads: ham, chicken,
>   egg, shrimp, etc.
> 1 3-ounce package cream cheese, softened
> 1 cup mayonnaise mixed with 1 tablespoon dry mustard
> Gherkins, stuffed green olives, fresh chopped parsley for
>   decoration

1. Divide croissant dough into thirds. Roll each piece into a rectangle ⅛–³⁄₁₆ inch thick, 9 inches long, and 7 inches wide.
2. Cut into 2 lengthwise strips, producing 2 strips 3½ inches wide and about 9 inches long.
3. Do the same with the other 2 pieces of dough. Place them on baking sheets about 1 inch apart.
4. Brush with egg glaze. Do not let it drip down the sides of dough because this might inhibit rising in the oven.
5. Bake in a preheated 450°F. oven for 10–12 minutes.
6. You can let the strips cool and freeze them. When ready to use, defrost and recrisp in a 400°F. oven for about 5–8 minutes.
7. Spread 1 cup of a filling on 1 strip. Place a second strip on top. Spread 1 cup of a second filling on this strip. Place a

third croissant strip on top. Repeat the process with the 3 remaining strips to make a second sandwich.

8. Combine cream cheese and mayonnaise mixture, stirring until smooth and of spreading consistency.

9. Frost the top layer with the combined cream cheese and mayonnaise mixture. Chill 15 minutes. Make ridges in frosting using tines of fork.

10. Decorate with gherkins, olives, parsley. Chill until ready to serve. Carefully cut each sandwich into 6 slices with a serrated knife.

Processor Mayonnaise for Layered Croissant Sandwiches

Makes 2 cups of mayonnaise (enough for 2 sandwiches)

1 egg at room temperature
2 egg yolks at room temperature
½ teaspoon salt
Dash Tabasco and freshly ground white pepper
2 tablespoons fresh lemon juice
1½ cups salad oil or a combination of excellent olive oil and salad oil
Wine vinegar or droplets of water (to lighten mixture at end; optional)

1. With the metal knife blade in food processor, place egg, yolks, salt, Tabasco, pepper, and lemon juice in processor container or blender. Process or blend for 1 minute.

2. With the machine running, slowly drizzle oil into the mixture through the feed tube, until the mixture begins to thicken. Then add oil in a slow, steady stream.

3. Adjust the seasoning, adding salt and pepper or vinegar or water as necessary. Mix with 2 quick on-off pulses.
   • *Refrigerate in an airtight container for as long as 4–5 days.*

FILLINGS FOR LAYERED CROISSANT SANDWICHES

Pecan-Chicken Salad

Makes 2½ cups of filling (enough for 2 sandwiches or 12 servings)

  1½ cups finely diced cooked chicken
  ⅓ cup minced celery
  ¼ cup ground pecans
  ⅙ cup mayonnaise
  ⅛ cup yogurt
  ½ teaspoon salt
  ¹⁄₁₆ teaspoon onion salt
  1 tablespoon lemon juice

1. Combine chicken, celery, pecans.
2. Mix the other ingredients in a bowl, then add to the chicken mixture.
3. Chill thoroughly.

Olive-Egg Salad

Makes about 2½ cups of filling (enough for 2 sandwiches or 12 servings)

  5 hard-boiled eggs, chopped fine
  ½ cup finely chopped pimiento-stuffed green olives
  3 tablespoons mayonnaise
  Salt to taste

1. Combine eggs and olives in a mixing bowl.
2. Add mayonnaise and mix well.
3. Taste and add salt, if needed
4. Chill thoroughly.

CROISSANT TARTS

Croissant dough, with its crispy lightness, becomes a beautiful croissant tart shell for creamy fillings such as the tuna filling recipe provided in this book. The dough can easily be rolled into a rectangle and then attractively slashed to give a peekaboo effect when folded over the filling. The filling stays moist but unsoggy even when the tart is prepared in advance and refrigerated for a day or when the tart is baked and then frozen for two months. The tart will thaw and recrisp in a half hour in a 400°F. oven. You can have an elegant luncheon or dinner entrée in your freezer for your next "command performance." Other fillings that work well in the tart are the Mexican, Mushroom, or Polish Sausage turnover fillings (see recipes). Simply double the recipes to fill 2 croissant tarts.

Tuna filling peeks out of slits in dough and cheese adds flavor to the flaky Croissant Tart.

Tuna Croissant Tarts

Makes 2 tarts (8 servings)

2 tablespoons chopped dill pickle
¼ cup chopped onion
1 tablespoon Dijon mustard
⅓ cup mayonnaise
1 9-ounce can water-packed tuna, drained
½ teaspoon dillweed
½ teaspoon dried savory
½ master recipe for Basic Butter Croissants
½ cup shredded Monterey Jack cheese
Egg glaze (1 egg beaten with 1 teaspoon water)
½ cup additional shredded Monterey Jack cheese (for top)
1 tablespoon sesame seed

1. Place pickle and onion in a bowl with mustard, mayonnaise, tuna, dillweed, and savory. Mix well.
2. Cut ½ Basic Butter Croissants recipe in half. Roll each half into a rectangle that measures 7″ x 9″.
3. Place rectangles 2 inches apart on a baking sheet.

4. Spoon tuna mixture in a 3-inch strip lengthwise down the center of each strip of dough.
5. Sprinkle ½ cup cheese over filling.
6. Make cuts 1 inch apart on each side of each rectangle just to the edge of the filling.
7. Fold strips across filling. Brush with egg glaze.

After placing tuna filling and cheese in center of tart rectangle, make slits about an inch apart from edge of dough toward filling. Then fold slits over top of filling.

8. Bake in the middle of a preheated 450°F. oven for 17 minutes.
9. Remove from oven. Lower temperature to 400°F. Sprinkle with ½ cup cheese and the sesame seed.
10. Return to the oven for 3 minutes.
11. Remove from the oven and cool for 5 minutes. Cut each tart into 4 slices and serve.

VIANDES EN CROUTE (MEATS WRAPPED IN CROISSANT DOUGH)

One of the most elegant uses of this dough is as an "en croûte" wrapping for meat in the manner of Beef Wellington. Croissant dough has all the advantages of puff pastry—its brown, crunchy, delicate look—but not the major disadvantage, which is a soggy, uncooked, doughy layer close to the meat. This wet, steamed layer results from moisture condensation as the meat cooks and cools. The thin, airy layer of croissant dough puffs in the oven and does not become wet. Even under the bottom of the meat, the dough crisps and browns evenly. The recipe included here uses a long chicken roll as a fresh variation of Beef Wellington, but you can surround a lovely piece of beef tenderloin coated with paté with croissant dough and produce the perfect Wellington.

"Wrapping up" meats and meat fillings in croissant dough dresses them up and seals in the juices while providing a crunchy, buttery covering.

Chicken en Croûte

Makes 8–10 servings

  1½ cups chopped cooked chicken
  5 ounces fresh or frozen spinach, cooked and well drained
  1 hard-boiled egg, chopped
  ¼ cup chopped *cornichons* or dill pickles
  2 tablespoons finely chopped celery
  1 tablespoon minced parsley
  Salt to taste
  2 tablespoons butter melted with ½ teaspoon dry mustard
  ½ master recipe for Basic Butter Croissants
  Egg glaze (1 egg beaten with 1 teaspoon water)
  1 cup yogurt blended with 2 tablespoons dill pickle juice
      and 1 teaspoon dillweed (for sauce)

1. Preheat oven to 425°F. Grease baking sheet.
2. In a bowl, combine chicken, spinach, egg, pickle, celery, parsley, salt.
3. Roll dough out to a 12" x 9" rectangle. Brush with butter-mustard mixture. Spread dough with chicken mixture, leaving a 1-inch margin all around.
4. From a long side, roll up. Pinch ends and seams to seal.
5. Place seam side down on baking sheet. Cut 2-inch slashes at 2-inch intervals across top of roll. Brush with egg glaze.
6. Bake for 18–20 minutes. Cool slightly.
7. Combine yogurt, pickle juice, and dillweed to pass with slices of roll or prepare Sauce 2 for Chicken en Croûte (see recipe below).
   - *You can bake the Chicken en Croûte ahead of time and reheat at 350°F. for 15–20 minutes in foil, leaving the top uncovered.*

Sauce 2 for Chicken en Croûte

Makes 2 cups of sauce (enough for 1 recipe Chicken en Croûte)

> 2 cups chicken stock
> 2 tablespoons butter
> 4 tablespoons all-purpose unbleached flour
> 1 egg yolk
> ½ cup Crème Fraîche 1 or 2 (see recipes) or cream
> ¼ teaspoon Tabasco (or to taste)
> 2 teaspoons tarragon
> Salt and white pepper to taste

1. Heat chicken stock to a boil in 1-quart saucepan.
2. In heavy-bottomed 2-quart saucepan, melt butter. Add flour and stir over medium-low heat for 2 minutes to cook the flour. The mixture should be foamy.
3. Remove 2-quart saucepan from heat and, while whisking, slowly add stock. Whisk until smooth. Add Tabasco and tarragon.
4. Simmer this sauce over low heat for about 30 minutes, stirring often.
5. Beat egg yolk slightly. Whisk in crème fraîche or cream. Slowly add sauce to yolk mixture, whisking steadily until all is added.
6. Return combined sauce to 2-quart saucepan. Boil, stirring, for one minute.
7. Season with salt and white pepper to taste.

6

Novel Croissant Forms

This versatile dough can become a number of lovely shapes to suit your needs. You can create smaller-sized croissants for first courses or desserts, brunch buffet croissant bites, or croissant rolls shaped like pinwheels with a dot of custard and jam in the center. You can even make a round inch-high sweet croissant cake called *kouign-aman,* a traditional regional French specialty found in the Breton region.

PETITS CROISSANTS

One recipe of croissant dough can be formed into 16 *petits croissants* according to the following directions. Petits croissants are delightful as a first course, a late-evening treat, or a party offering. The petits croissants can be filled with any of the sweet and savory fillings listed in previous chapters. I have also included three savory fillings that seem to work particularly well with these tiny treats.

Basic Petits Croissants

Makes 16 4-inch croissants

1 master recipe for Basic Butter Croissants
Egg glaze (1 egg beaten with 1 teaspoon water)

1. Begin after step 23 in the master recipe. Place the dough on a floured cold surface with the flap on your right. Roll the dough into a rectangle 24 inches long and 3–4 inches wide. Cut in half horizontally to make two 12-inch-long pieces. Refrigerate 1 piece.
2. Roll 1 piece into a rectangle 16 inches long and 4 inches wide. Place a ruler next to the dough. Using a knife or scraper, make 3 horizontal cuts in the dough at the 4-inch mark, 8-inch mark, and 12-inch mark on the ruler. This creates four 4-inch squares.
3. Using a knife or scraper, cut each square in half diagonally (from corner to corner), creating 2 triangles out of each square.
4. Place each triangle with the base down (south) and the point up (north) on the work surface. Using your fingers, stretch and pull the left (west) corner and the right (east) corner of the base out about a half inch on each side, widening by 1 inch altogether. Elongate the triangle height to about 5 inches by stretching triangle lengthwise.
5. Roll up as in step 28 of the master recipe and continue to form all 16 small croissants as described in the master recipe.
6. Follow steps 31 and 32 in the master recipe concerning rising and preheating oven. Paint with egg glaze just before baking.
7. Bake on a buttered baking sheet in the middle of a preheated 450°F. oven for 5 minutes. Reduce heat to 375°F. and bake about 10 more minutes. Smaller croissants will bake slightly faster than larger ones.
8. To cool and freeze the croissants, follow step 35 and the concluding tip in the master recipe.

Ham-and-Cheese-Filled Croissants

Makes 16 4-inch croissants

> 1 master recipe for **Basic Butter Croissants**
> 5 tablespoons plus 1 teaspoon **Dijon mustard** (16 teaspoons, 1 per croissant)
> 16 thin slices **Danish or fine boiled ham, cut to fit into croissant triangle**
> 16 thin slices **Gruyère or Swiss cheese, cut to fit into croissant triangle**
> **Egg glaze (1 egg beaten with 1 teaspoon water)**

1. Form 16 dough triangles as in steps 1–4 in the master recipe for Basic Petits Croissants.
2. Spread 1 teaspoon mustard on each triangle.

While you don't have to cut ham and cheese into triangles, this way there is no leakage.

3. Place ham slice and cheese slice on mustard.
4. Form, let rise, paint with egg glaze, and bake as directed in master recipe.
5. Cool slightly on a rack. Paint with Honey Glaze (see recipe) if desired.

Egg Roll Croissants.

Egg Roll Croissants

Makes 1 cup of filling (enough for 16 4-inch croissants)

½ cup uncooked chicken, cut into pieces
½ cup fresh or canned bean sprouts
2 dried mushrooms, rehydrated and drained
1 tablespoon fresh parsley (about 4 sprigs)
2 tablespoons shallots (about ⅛ cup)
1 small clove garlic, peeled
¼ teaspoon ginger
¼ teaspoon cornstarch
1½ teaspoons soy sauce
¼ teaspoon salt
⅛ teaspoon freshly ground white pepper
1 master recipe for Basic Butter Croissants
Egg glaze (1 egg beaten with 1 teaspoon water)

1. In a food processor or blender, chop chicken, bean sprouts, mushrooms, parsley, and shallots. While machine is running, drop garlic cloves into machine.
2. Place ginger, cornstarch, and soy sauce in skillet and mix.
3. Add chopped ingredients. Cook over medium-high heat, stirring often, for 7 minutes. Add salt and pepper. Cool 5 minutes. Meanwhile, preheat oven to 450°F.
4. Roll dough into small-sized croissant triangles.
5. Place 1 tablespoon of filling in the center of each triangle and roll up.
6. Form, let rise, paint with egg glaze, and bake as directed in master recipe.
7. Serve warm with a sweet and sour sauce and/or a mustard sauce.

Pepperoni and Mozzarella Croissants

Makes 8 small croissants

> ½ **master recipe for Basic Butter Croissants**
> **24 1½-inch-diameter slices of pepperoni** *or* **8 3-inch**
>   **diameter slices**
> **8 thin slices mozzarella cheese**
> **Egg glaze (1 egg beaten with 1 teaspoon water)**

1. Using ½ master recipe, form 8 dough triangles following the recipe for Basic Petits Croissants.
2. Place pepperoni in center of each triangle.
3. Top each with cheese slice.
4. Form, let rise, paint with egg glaze, and bake as directed in master recipe.
5. To cool and freeze croissants, follow step 35 and the concluding tip in the master recipe.

Croissant Brunch Shapes.

CROISSANT BRUNCH SHAPES

Croissant dough can be shaped into a wide variety of tiny, tempting treats. Tiny croissants filled with a teaspoon or so of a sweet filling look very attractive on a brunch buffet table. Or you can braid small strips of dough and top off the bread with a sweet topping. Pudgy little pouches of croissant dough can enclose a sweet filling. A little wreath or snail layered with a colorful filling outshines any traditional coffee cake. One dough recipe can produce 24 bite-sized croissant shapes, which can be frozen for later use.

Basic Croissant Brunch Shapes

Makes about 24 petits brunch croissants

> **1 master recipe for Basic Butter Croissants**
> **Custard, chocolate, or sweet filling (see recipes)**
> **Egg glaze (1 egg beaten with 1 teaspoon water)**
> **Sweet glaze (see recipes)**

1. After step 23 in the master recipe, cut dough in half. Refrigerate half.
2. Roll half of the dough into any-size square or rectangle ⅛ inch thick.

3. Cut out pieces to make the following desired shapes:

Braid
 a. Cut a rectangle 1½ inches wide and 3–4 inches long.
 b. Cut 3 lengthwise strips ½ inch thick.
 c. Braid the 3 strips.

Pouch
 a. Cut a small 2-inch square.
 b. Place 1 teaspoon of filling in the center.
 c. Bring 2 opposite or diagonal corners up and over filling and pinch tips together. Bring 2 remaining opposite corners up and over filling, pinching the 4 tips together to form a pouch.

Wreath
 a. Cut a 4-inch square of dough.
 b. Spread on a thick layer of filling.
 c. Roll up and pinch seam.
 d. Curve roll into a doughnut or circle and pinch or seal two ends to make a completely closed, smooth circle.
 e. Make slits ½ inch apart, cutting almost completely through dough, and fan segments attractively to expose the interior swirl design.

Snails
 a. Cut a 4-inch square of dough.
 b. Spread on a thick layer of filling.
 c. Roll up and pinch seam.
 d. Cut into ½-inch snails and place cut side down on baking sheet.

4. Paint shapes with egg glaze and bake on a buttered baking sheet in a preheated 450°F. oven for 8–10 minutes.
5. While warm or at room temperature, the shapes may be glazed.

 ● *The braid shapes taste best with a very sweet glaze since they have no sweet filling inside.*

These flaky croissant pinwheels offer a hint of sweetness in the custard and preserves centers.

PINWHEEL CROISSANTS

Pinwheel croissants about 3 inches in size, sprinkled with powdered sugar or painted with Apricot Glaze, are delicious for breakfast, at tea time, or for dessert. Forming them is simple, and as with all the croissant recipes, they freeze and recrisp beautifully!

Pinwheel Croissants

Makes 12 pinwheel croissants

   1 master recipe for **Basic Butter Croissants**
   1 cup **Crème Pâtissière 1 or 2 (see recipes)**
   Red currant jelly or apricot jam (optional)
   Egg glaze (1 egg beaten with 1 teaspoon water)
   Powdered sugar

1. Roll dough out to form an 18″ x 6″ rectangle. Cut in half horizontally. Refrigerate half.
2. Cut piece in half vertically creating 2 9″ x 3″ strips. Cut

each strip into thirds horizontally, creating 3 3″ squares from each strip.

3. Place a teaspoon of custard in the center of each square and about a teaspoon of jelly on top of custard. You can put in more custard, if you wish.

4. Cut from each corner toward the center, continuing almost to the filling.

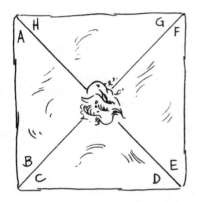

Step 4

After placing a teaspoon of custard and preserves filling in the center of the pinwheel square, slits are cut diagonally from corners almost to the filling.

5. Moisten all 8 corner tips with water. Lift corner A all the way over the center, covering the custard. Skip corner B. Lift C over the center and press lightly to make corner stick. Continue with corners E and then G, pressing the tips together. Repeat with the remaining squares. Repeat steps 2–5 with the other dough half.

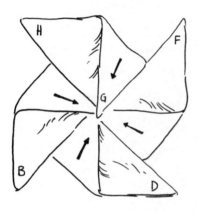

Step 5

Every other split corner is folded over the center filling to create the pinwheel effect.

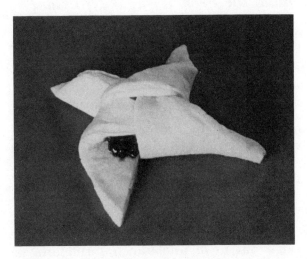

The finished pinwheel must rise before baking.

6. Let rolls rise and puff for about 1½ hours. Brush with egg glaze and bake in the middle of a preheated 450°F. oven for about 10–15 minutes, until golden brown.
7. Remove from oven. Place on a rack to cool. When cool, sprinkle with powdered sugar through a sieve.

KOUIGN-AMAN, THE FRENCH SUGAR CROISSANT CAKE

The French Sugar Croissant Cake is a paradox: it is a round 1- to 1½-inch-high cake, buttery, sugary, and soft in the center, but crispy and brown on the outside. One half of the croissant master recipe makes one cake that serves eight. However, you must remember to make only *two turns* with the croissant dough before proceeding with this recipe, because more turns are made with the addition of granulated sugar. Accompanied by lingonberries, it is a beautiful coffee cake and so simple to prepare!

Kouign-aman, the French Sugar Croissant

Makes 1 9-inch cake (about 8 servings)

> **½ master recipe for Basic Butter Croissants (prepared only up to 2 turns, not 4)**
> **½ cup sugar, plus a little more for final sprinkling**

1. Beginning with the third turn, roll ½ croissant recipe into an 8″ x 12″ rectangle. Sprinkle the upper two-thirds of the dough with half the sugar. Fold as for a business letter. Give dough a quarter-turn. Roll out into an 8″ x 12″ rectangle again, sprinkling with remaining sugar. Fold as before.
2. Chill for 1 hour.
3. Roll dough out to fit into 9-inch springform pan with tinfoil wrapped around bottom. Butter the pan.
4. Set the dough in the pan and let rise for 1 hour.
5. Preheat oven to 400°F.
6. When the cake has risen slightly, sprinkle with a little sugar and bake for 30–35 minutes, or until golden brown and puffed. Serve hot or lukewarm.

7

Puff Pastry

French puff pastry was probably the inspiration for French
bakers when they overhauled the Austrian kipfel, brought to
France by Marie Antoinette, and created the croissant. Both
puff pastry and croissants utilize almost equal proportions of
butter and flour, rolled and folded to form layers that puff and
crisp in the oven. So it seems only fitting to include in this
book an easy preparation for puff pastry and several attractive
uses for it.

Puff pastry is a blend of flour, salt, and ice water into which
cold butter is incorporated so that, through rolling and folding
the dough, layers of dough and butter are created. During
baking the air incorporated into the dough during rolling and
folding expands, producing a puffed, risen, crispy, layered
pastry.

The master recipe for puff pastry couldn't be simpler.
Chunks of butter are added to flour *before* six turns are made.
During the first turn you must contend with a crumbly mass,
but through subsequent turns you will create a pliable dough
that produces flaky, puffed pastry. These puff pastry recipes
waste nothing! Even the wet interiors from the cooked appetizer shells become part of a simple puffed cheese ramekin,
similar to a soufflé but easier to make. Scraps of uncooked

pastry become classic French cookies called *palmiers*. Finally, if you love chocolate as I do, you'll enjoy making chocolate puff pastry. You can freeze raw dough for a year! You can also cook, freeze, thaw, and recrisp this dough just as you do for croissants.

Basic Puff Pastry

Makes 2 10″ x 15″ tart shells *or* 1 8- to 9-inch Pithiviers *or* 50 appetizer shells (petites bouchées)

> 3 cups unbleached all-purpose flour (plus 1 cup used during the turns)
> 1 cup plain bleached cake flour
> 6¼ sticks chilled unsalted butter, cut into ½-inch dice
> 1½ teaspoons salt
> 1 cup ice water aciduated with ½ teaspoon lemon juice

1. Prepare puff pastry: Place flours in bowl. Add butter and salt. Blend until butter forms lumps the size of cranberries. Blend in just enough water to wet dough so it will mass.
2. Turn dough out onto a lightly floured cold work surface. Push, pat, and roll dough into an 18″ x 6″ rectangle. Lightly flour surface, and with a pastry scraper to help you, flip the bottom of the rectangle up over the middle and then flip the top down to cover it, as though folding a business letter. The pastry will be a crumbly mess!
3. Push off work area. Resprinkle with flour and replace dough so the flap is on your right. Roll dough out again into a rectangle about 18″ x 6″, sprinkle with more flour, and fold in three. You have now completed 2 turns. *Each turn is made up of a roll-out and a fold-up.* Do 2 more turns, incorporating a sprinkling of flour as you roll and fold. After your last fold, place the folded dough in plastic wrap and in a plastic bag for 40 minutes. Do 2 more turns, incorporating the remaining flour from the additional 1 cup. Let the dough rest for another 30 minutes or, better yet, overnight.
    *   *You can freeze this dough for years!*

Note: Blending can be done by hand (with your fingers) but it does get messy and tedious. I suggest you use a heavy-duty upright mixer with a flat paddle; I've found the Kitchen Aid machine to be the best by far. Do *not* use a food processor.

Petites Bouchées (Puff Pastry Appetizer Shells)

Makes 20 appetizer shells

Puffed little shells hollowed out and filled with a rich cheese filling create "little mouthfuls," appetizers everyone will rave about.

⅓ **Basic Puff Pastry recipe**
Egg glaze (1 egg beaten with 1 teaspoon water)

1. Roll dough into a ¼-inch-thick piece and cut out 20 circles with a 2-inch round fluted cutter.
2. With a 1-inch cutter, press the outline of a lid into the top center of each 2-inch circle, going ⅛ inch deep. Refrigerate at least 1 hour on a baking sheet sprinkled with water. Glaze and bake in a preheated 450°F. oven for about 12 minutes, until puffed and browned.

Quarter-inch-thick puff pastry dough will triple in size during baking.

Pastry lids and uncooked interior of the appetizer shell are removed while still warm.

3. While still warm, remove the pastry lids and any uncooked pastry from the interior. Save the gooey interior for Cheese Ramekin (see recipe).
   - *At this point you can freeze shells wrapped in foil. Thaw by placing shells on a baking sheet in a 400° F. oven for about 5 minutes.*
5. Whenever you are ready to fill the shells and do the final baking, preheat oven to 450° F.
6. Fill cooked shells with a very stiff paste (see following recipe), using a small spoon or pastry bag.
7. Bake in the upper middle of the oven for 8–10 minutes, until cheese filling is slightly golden.
8. Place on a tray and serve.

Using a pastry bag or a spoon, place thick filling in hollowed appetizer shell.

Petites Bouchées Filling

Makes about 1½ cups of filling (enough to fill 20 appetizer shells)

4½ teaspoons minced shallots
1 small clove garlic, mashed
1½ teaspoons butter
½ cup dry vermouth
½ cup evaporated milk
½ cup all-purpose flour
2 tablespoons butter
2 large eggs
Salt and pepper to taste
Pinch nutmeg and cayenne
4 ounces grated Swiss cheese
2 ounces grated Parmesan
3-4 tablespoons Milnot or Crème Fraîche 1 or 2 (see recipes), if needed

1. Using an enameled or heavy-bottomed 1-quart saucepan, cook shallots and garlic slowly in 1½ teaspoons butter for a moment. Add wine, raise heat, and boil down rapidly until wine is reduced to ¼ cup.
2. Gradually beat driblets of evaporated milk mixed with the ¼ cup garlic and wine flavoring into the flour in a heavy-bottomed 2-quart saucepan, adding ¾ cup altogether and beating to a smooth consistency. Add butter and set pan over medium heat, stirring.
3. As mixture begins to boil it will get lumpy. Remove from heat and beat to smooth it out, using a wire whisk.
4. One by one, beat in eggs, then bring to a boil, beating constantly. *Sauce must be a thick paste.*
5. Remove from heat and season with salt, pepper, nutmeg, and cayenne. Cool for a few minutes.
6. Fold in cheese. Fold in just enough Crème Fraîche 1 or 2 or Milnot to soften it slightly; sauce must hold its shape when mounded in a spoon.
    • *You can freeze this paste.*
7. Press a sheet of plastic wrap over the surface of the sauce to prevent a skin or crust from forming.

Variations

Decrease cheese by half and add ham or diced sautéed mushrooms.

- *You can bake shells, fill, and freeze in foil so that you only need to bake a few minutes and serve when company comes. You can place them directly in the oven on opened foil to eliminate cleanup.*

Cheese Ramekin (Using Uncooked Bouchées Interiors)

Makes 4–6 servings

A puffy soufflélike cheese pudding is a creative alternative to potatoes when served with any roast or chicken.

⅓–½ cup pressed, slightly warm, uncooked insides from
    bouchees
1 cup milk
2 large eggs
⅛ teaspoon nutmeg
⅛ teaspoon cayenne
⅛ teaspoon salt
5 tablespoons fresh grated Parmesan cheese

1. Puree uncooked pastry and milk for a minute, until smoothed completely. Add eggs, seasonings, and cheese and puree 5 seconds.
2. Pour into buttered baking dish.
   - *You can refrigerate until the next day, if desired.*
3. Preheat oven to 375°F. Bake about half an hour until nicely puffed and browned. Serve immediately in place of potatoes.
   - *You may freeze uncooked interiors scooped out of bouchées (appetizer shells) until you are ready to make this ramekin. Place interior pieces in the oven until thawed and warm before proceeding with this recipe.*

Le Pithiviers (Puff Pastry with Almond Cream Filling)

Makes 1 8- to 9-inch tart

Two puff pastry layers hold a ball of almond butter cream, a rich, sweet, light gift from the small French town of Pithiviers.

⅓ cup sugar
½ stick (2 ounces) soft butter
1 large egg
½ cup (2½ ounces) ground blanched almonds
¼ teaspoon almond extract
¼ teaspoon vanilla extract
1 tablespoon cognac
1 teaspoon orange liqueur
⅓ cup powdered sugar (for caramelizing top at end of baking)
1 master recipe for Basic Puff Pastry
Egg glaze (1 egg beaten with 1 teaspoon water)

1. Beat sugar and butter until soft and fluffy, using a wooden spoon. Add egg, almonds, extracts, cognac, and orange liqueur. Beat to blend. Place in a small bowl. Cover and freeze for 30 minutes, or until very firm.

2. Roll puff pastry into a 14″ x 8″ rectangle. Cut in half crosswise and refrigerate half. Roll remaining half into a 9½-inch square that is ⅜ inch thick. Center an 8-inch cake pan on dough. Cut out an 8-inch circle. Sprinkle cold water on a baking sheet. Roll the circle up on the rolling pin and unroll on the baking sheet. Refrigerate. Roll second half of dough. Cut into an 8-inch circle ⅜ inch thick. Place on wax paper and refrigerate both circles for 20 minutes.

3. Remove baking sheet with circle on it. Push the circle with fingers from center outward to make a 9-inch circle. Make the center thinner than the circumference to ensure that it will bake through completely. Place the firm almond cream in the center, making a blob about 4 inches in diameter.

4. Rapidly roll out the second disk, enlarging it to 9 inches.

Paint the circumference of the bottom disk with cold water, roll the top disk up on the pin, and unroll over the bottom disk. Seal the two layers first by pressing all around the circumference of the almond cream with the side of your hand, pressing hard to seal. Make a little hole in the top of the dough down into the cream so air can escape during baking. Press dough firmly with the flat of your fingers from the edge of the cream outward to the edge of the dough to seal. You want to hold almond cream in the center so it won't leak out the sides. Chill again for 30 minutes.

5. Preheat the oven to 450° F. Remove pastry from the refrigerator. Center an 8-inch cake pan over the pastry. You should have about half an inch of dough protruding all around. With a sharp knife, make a decorative edge by removing little *V* shapes of dough about every 2 inches. Press the cake pan down to make an indentation and another seal. Press the tines of a fork held upright outside the edging all around as a final seal.

    • *You can freeze the pastry at this point.*

6. Paint the top of the pastry with egg glaze, but don't drip egg down the sides or pastry can't puff. Insert a buttered metal funnel into the air hole. Push way down into the almond cream. Paint with a second coating of glaze. With a knife point, make a decorative design, cutting ⅛ inch deep into dough.

7. Place pastry in the lower middle of the preheated oven. Bake 20 minutes, until triple in height. Lower heat to 400° F. and bake another 25 minutes. Sprinkle a ⅛-inch layer of powdered sugar over the top and bake for 3 minutes, checking often, at 500° F. in the upper third of the oven. Take the funnel out of the center for this final caramelizing of the top.

    • *You can freeze the cooked pastry. Thaw for 30–40 minutes in a 350° F. oven, uncovered.*

Puff Pastry Fruit Tart

Makes 1 10″ x 15″ tart

A free-form puff pastry frame, the perfect setting for any fruit filling, pretty as a picture.

½ **Basic Puff Pastry recipe**
½ **cup Apricot Glaze (see recipe)**
1½–3 **cups Vanilla Crème Pâtissière (see recipe)**
2 **pints fresh strawberries, hulled, or any soft fruit of your choice such as bananas, berries, or grapes**

1. Roll dough out on a lightly floured surface so that it is 14 inches long and no less than ¼ inch thick.
2. Cut off 4 strips from the perimeter of the rectangle, about 1¼ inches wide. Trim strips so that they are about ¾ inch wide. Refrigerate strips.
3. Roll remainder of dough into a 12″ x 14″ rectangle ⅛ inch thick. Roll it up on your pin and gently unroll on a greased jelly roll pan. Trim edges evenly.
4. With cold water, paint a perimeter about ¾ inch thick and press the refrigerated strips firmly on, creating a frame. Trim again to even all the edges and sides.
5. While pressing down on the top of the strip with fingers, press the outside in toward the center of the tart with the tines of a fork held upright. Cut a decorative design on the top of the strips. Refrigerate tart for 1 hour.
6. Preheat oven to 450°F. Prick bottom of tart at ¼-inch intervals with a fork. Place a sheet of aluminum foil inside tart and pour in weights (rice, beans, aluminum pie weights).
7. Bake for 20 minutes. Remove foil and weights. Prick bottom again with a fork. Lower heat to 400°F. Bake an additional 5–8 minutes, until nicely browned.
8. Remove from oven. Let cool 10 minutes. Slide onto rack.
   - *You can freeze this and have it ready when you are.*

9. Paint tart with warm Apricot Glaze and let rest 5 minutes to set.
10. Spread about a ½-inch-thick layer of Crème Pâtissière over tart bottom.
11. Arrange fresh hulled strawberries close together and pointed ends up in the cream. Spoon remaining warm Apricot Glaze over berries.
12. Refrigerate until serving time.

These crisp, palm-shaped classic French cookies, palmiers, are elegant and light served alone or with ice cream.

Palmiers (Using Puff Pastry to Make Cookies)

Glazed in caramelized sugar, palmiers are crispy cookies shaped like little palm leaves or butterflies.

Scraps of pastry dough
Granulated sugar
Powdered sugar

1. Roll dough into a rectangle on a rolling surface sprinkled generously with granulated sugar.
2. Sprinkle the top side of the dough generously with powdered sugar.
3. Fold dough in half to center, and fold over again, making a double roll on the left side and right side, meeting in the center.
4. Press firmly with a rolling pin. Fold as if closing a book. Press firmly again with pin.
5. Make horizontal slices about ¼ or ½ inch thick.
6. Bake on an unbuttered cookie sheet in a preheated 450°F. oven (upper middle rack) for 6 minutes. Flip, sprinkle with

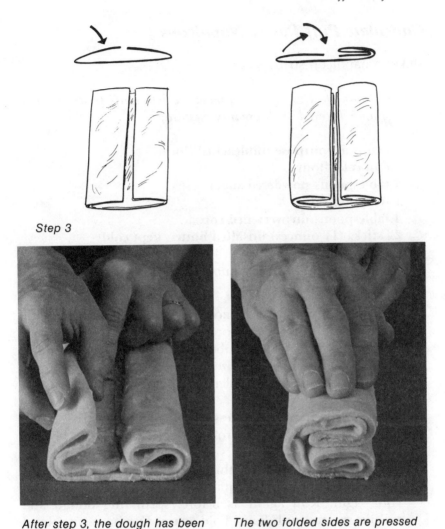

Step 3

After step 3, the dough has been folded in half to center twice.

The two folded sides are pressed together in step 4.

powdered sugar, and bake 3 more minutes. You can continue sprinkling and turning, depending on how crispy and golden you prefer your cookies.

7. Let cookies cool on a rack. Don't let them touch each other until cooled or they may stick together.

Chocolate Puff Pastry Napoleons

Makes 6 napoleon strips

True "chocoholics" will appreciate crispy puff pastry with a cocoa flavor layered with creamy custard.

1½ cups all-purpose unbleached flour
½ cup cake flour
4 tablespoons powdered sugar
1 teaspoon salt
4 tablespoons unsweetened cocoa
2¾ sticks (11 ounces) unsalted butter, kept cold
½ cup ice water
About ⅔ cup all-purpose unbleached flour (to use in
     rolling)

1. In a large mixing bowl, place flours, sugar, salt, cocoa. Stir together with a wooden spoon.
2. Cut butter into ½-inch cubes and add to flour mixture. Blend, leaving butter the size of cranberries (see note).
3. Add water and continue blending just until dough begins to mass a little.
4. Remove from bowl and press together using pastry scraper.
5. Flour rolling surface and roll dough into a 12- to 14-inch rectangle (about 5–6 inches wide). Flour surface and fold bottom third up and top third down as in folding a business letter. Give dough a quarter-turn so the flap side is on your right. Roll again as before, sprinkling dough and rolling surface with flour. Fold again. You have completed 2 turns (a turn is a roll-and-fold).
6. Do 2 more turns. Take folded dough, wrap in plastic, and refrigerate 40 minutes. Then do 2 more turns. Refrigerate again for 30 minutes before forming or freeze.
7. Roll dough into a square about 19 inches and ¼ –¹⁄₁₆ inch thick. Cut into 6 pieces and place on 2 moistened baking sheets. Cut off any unstraight sides and overlaps. Save these scraps for cookies. Pierce surface with fork tines, very close together. Refrigerate for 40 minutes.
8. Preheat oven to 450°F. Place 2 sheets in upper and lower

thirds of oven. Bake 10 minutes. Reduce heat to 375°F. and switch sheets. Bake about 10–15 more minutes. Remove napoleons from sheets and let cool on wire racks.

- *You can freeze these in foil. You can then reheat them in open foil in a 350°F. oven for about 5 minutes to thaw and recrisp.*

Note: Blending can be done by hand (with your fingers) but it does get messy and tedious. I suggest you use a heavy duty upright mixer with a flat paddle; I've found the Kitchen Aid machine to be the best by far. Do *not* use a food processor.

Assembling Chocolate Puff Pastry Napoleons

Makes 7–8 pastries

> **3 strips Chocolate Puff Pastry (see recipe)**
> **Apricot Glaze (see recipe)**
> **1 cup Vanilla Crème Pâtissière (see recipe)**
> **Powdered sugar (for sprinkling on top; optional)**
> **Cocoa (for sprinkling on top; optional)**

1. Paint side of the first rectangle of puff pastry with a little Apricot Glaze. Put half of the Crème Pâtissière on the rectangle and spread evenly.
2. Paint both sides of the second rectangle of puff pastry with glaze and place on top of Crème Pâtissière. Put remaining half of the custard on the second rectangle.
3. Paint 1 side of the third rectangle and place glaze side down on custard.
4. If you sprinkle the top with powdered sugar and cocoa, you have created mille feuilles, not true napoleons. However, anyone tasting this dessert has met his Waterloo!
5. Arrange on a serving tray and chill for an hour.
   - *These are best fresh, but you can refrigerate them for 3 days.*
6. Serve by cutting vertically into 7–8 small layered pastries. A very sharp carving knife or large serrated knife cuts cleanly.

8

Chocolate Lover's Croissants

Because I am such a dedicated "chocoholic," I had to create a chocolate croissant for myself. The basic techniques you have already learned are applied in this slight variation of the master recipe for Basic Butter Croissants. Cocoa and powdered sugar are added to the dry ingredients. Additional sugar creates a slightly less pliable dough that is more difficult to roll. But if the dough is kept cold, you will have only minor difficulty. The filling is a fudge lover's delight and my favorite flavor finale.

Chocolate Lover's Croissants

Makes 12 croissants

For Proofing

    2 teaspoons active dry yeast
    2 teaspoons granulated sugar
    1 teaspoon all-purpose unbleached flour
    3 tablespoons warm (100° F.) water

    1¾ cups all-purpose unbleached flour
    ½ teaspoon salt
    4 tablespoons unsweetened cocoa
    4 tablespoons powdered sugar

These Chocolate Lover's Croissants are a triple treat with chocolate dough, thick fudge filling, and shiny chocolate glaze.

> 2 tablespoons granulated sugar mixed with ⅔ cup warm
>   (100°F.) milk
> 1 teaspoon peanut oil
> 1¼ sticks cold unsalted butter
> 1 cup Fudge Filling (see recipe below)
> Egg glaze (1 egg beaten with 1 teaspoon water)
> Chocolate Glaze (see recipe)

1. Proof yeast as in the master recipe for Basic Butter Croissants.
2. Measure flour, salt, cocoa, and powdered sugar into a bowl.
3. Heat milk and sugar just to 100°F. Add milk to flour mixture with peanut oil and proofed yeast.
4. Follow directions in master recipe, steps 5–27, using 1¼ sticks butter instead of 1½.
5. Place 1 tablespoon of Fudge Filling in each croissant center, spreading a little but not extending to narrow point end.
6. Roll up and let rise as directed in steps 28–31.
7. Fifteen minutes before baking, preheat oven to 425°F. and place the rack in the middle of the oven.
8. Brush croissants twice with egg glaze. Bake 5 minutes and then reduce heat to 375°F. Continue baking 10–15 minutes more.
9. Remove croissants to a cooling rack.
10. Serve warm or cool. For a triple chocolate treat, pour Chocolate Glaze over croissants before serving.

Fudge Filling

Makes 1¼ cups (enough for 12 croissants)

> 2 squares (2 ounces) semisweet chocolate
> 2 squares (2 ounces) unsweetened chocolate
> 6 tablespoons Crème Fraîche 1 or 2 (see recipes)
> ½ cup sweetened condensed milk
> ¼ teaspoon orange extract or almond extract
> 1 tablespoon orange liqueur or rum
> 3 tablespoons Apricot Glaze (see recipe)

1. Slowly melt chocolates, Crème Fraîche, and milk in a 1-quart saucepan, stirring constantly with a rubber spatula.
2. Add extract, liqueur or rum, and Apricot Glaze, stirring until smooth.
3. Allow to thicken in the refrigerator or at room temperature for easier spreading.
   - *You can freeze this topping, defrost at room temperature, and use whenever desired.*

Index